Practical
Statistics

Thi

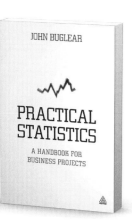

Practical Statistics

A handbook for business projects

John Buglear

KoganPage

LONDON   PHILADELPHIA   NEW DELHI

First published in Great Britain and the United States in 2014 by Kogan Page Limited

2nd Floor, 45 Gee Street
London EC1V 3RS
United Kingdom
www.koganpage.com

1518 Walnut Street, Suite 1100
Philadelphia PA 19102
USA

4737/23 Ansari Road
Daryaganj
New Delhi 110002
India

© John Buglear, 2014

ISBN   978 0 7494 6846 0
E-ISBN   978 0 7494 6847 7

British Library Cataloguing-in-Publication Data

A CIP record for this book is available from the British Library.

Library of Congress Cataloging-in-Publication Data

Buglear, John.
    Practical statistics : a handbook for business projects / John Buglear.
        pages cm
    ISBN 978-0-7494-6846-0 (pbk.) – ISBN 978-0-7494-6847-7 (ebook)   1. Commercial statistics.
2. Statistics.   3. Management–Statistical methods.   I. Title.
    HF1017.B84 2014
    519.5–dc23
                                                                        2013032120

Typeset by Graphicraft Limited, Hong Kong
Print production managed by Jellyfish
Printed and bound by CPI Group (UK) Ltd, Croydon, CR0 4YY

CONTENTS

Introduction

Let me start with a few questions. Are you a postgraduate or final year under-graduate? Do you have to do a research project or dissertation? Will you be analysing data for your project? Do you need to use quantitative research methods to analyse your data? Is the answer to each question 'Yes'? Then this book is for you.

OK. Now I would like to tell you something about me. My name is John Buglear and I work at Nottingham Business School. I teach research methods to under-graduate and postgraduate students. My specialism is quantitative research methods, or what I prefer to call statistics. Most of my colleagues may be experts in HR, marketing or strategy but don't know much about statistics. They supervise student research projects in their own fields but few can advise the students they supervise on the statistical analysis that can be an important part of the project. In these situations supervisors ask me to do this. With my guidance the statistical work students produce often greatly impresses their supervisors and examiners.

There are a few very important basic things that you need to know about statis-tics. Your supervisor probably assumes you know these already. You may not, or you may have studied them some time ago. The first chapter of this book covers these essentials. The second chapter shows you methods of analysing just one variable. The third chapter shows you how to investigate connections between two variables. The fourth chapter covers the analysis of relationships between more than two variables. The fifth chapter demonstrates less structured ways of exploring connec-tions within sets of variables.

Using statistical analysis is like cooking. Some things are easy to cook. To cook an egg you need something to cook it in. It is cooking only one type of food but you do need the correct tool: a saucepan if you want a boiled egg, a frying pan if you want a fried egg. The statistical analysis in Chapter 2 is rather like cooking an egg: it requires just one ingredient – a single set of figures such as the ages of a group of customers – but you can 'cook' it in different ways, perhaps a block diagram or an average. Because this type of analysis is applied to one set of figures, values of one variable, it is called *univariate* analysis.

An egg may not be enough; you may want something to go with it, such as bacon. Bacon and eggs is quite a popular dish. Many people think the flavours go together well. The statistical analysis in Chapter 3 is used to analyse values of two variables that we suspect complement each other, like eggs complement bacon. We may want to analyse the ages of customers with the amounts they spend on a product. This type of analysis is called *bivariate* because it is applied to two variables.

Cooking is often more complicated and involves recipes with more than two ingredients. The statistical analysis in Chapter 4 is used to analyse more than two variables. Because it involves multiple variables it is called *multivariate* analysis. A recipe is a structured set of instructions that tell us the composition of the dish and sequence to follow. The techniques in Chapter 4 are like recipes, for instance there are guidelines on the role of different types of variable.

Professional chefs approach cooking in a much more creative way. They experiment with different combinations of ingredients. The statistical analysis in Chapter 5 is like this. The methods in it are more exploratory but like the methods in Chapter 4 they are multivariate. They are used to investigate relationships between many variables, just like a chef explores how different foods go together.

If you have followed my analogy so far you have probably noticed I have left out Chapter 1. Before you can cook you need to know how to use a kitchen. What is in Chapter 1 is equivalent to that: what you need to know before you start any serious statistical analysis. An important part of Chapter 1 is the distinction between *metric* and *non-metric* data. Metric data is based on measurement; non-metric data is based on categorization. The techniques you can use for your project depend on which type of data you have.

The basic structure of the book is shown here as a flowchart. To help you use this book more efficiently, each section of each chapter opens with *The essentials,* which tells you what is in the section. After *The essentials* the full content of the section is headed *Tell me more.* You can skip this if you know the subject of that section, or you don't need to use it. To show you how to use the more sophisticated methods I have used examples to illustrate them.

Project work is a very important part of your higher education. It is where you take charge: you decide what to investigate and how to do it. The correct use of data analysis can make an ordinary project into a good one and make a good one great. To help you make the most of your work I have included a short closing section giving advice on discussion and presentation of data analysis. To return to my cooking analogy this Coda is the equivalent of presenting the food on the plate. Relatively small things like garnish and layout can make a dish much more appetizing and in the same way there are things you can do to give your work more impact and get the credit for it that it deserves. You would probably be surprised to learn how often good data analysis is under-rewarded because supervisors, examiners and viva panel members haven't got enough on what they need to know to appreciate how good the analysis really is.

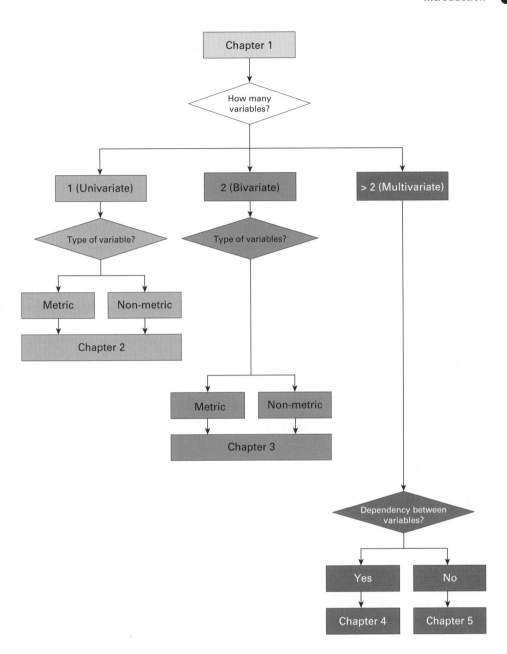

What you need to know before you start analysing data

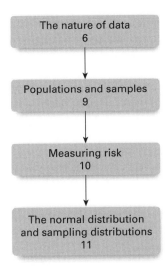

The nature of data
6

Populations and samples
9

Measuring risk
10

The normal distribution
and sampling distributions
11

Topics in this chapter:

- The nature of data and possible sources of data. Data is the raw material for the techniques covered in the chapters that follow this one.

- To use your data effectively you need to know how it relates to the broad context of your investigation. The concepts of population and sample are important for this.

- Generalizing findings from a sample to a population involves a certain amount of risk. Understanding how risk is measured enables you to do this scientifically.

- Statistical distributions, or patterns of variation are important conceptual ingredients of statistical techniques. The normal distribution is the most important: it underpins many sampling distributions, which are key links between sample results and population characteristics.

What is data?

The essentials

The word 'data' comes from the Latin word *datum* which means a given thing. There are different types of data. The most important distinction is between data that can only be arranged by category, 'categorical' data, and data that is based on measuring on a scale, 'measurement' data. Measurement data is also known as 'metric' or 'quantitative' data and categorical data is also known as 'non-metric' or 'qualitative' data. In this book I use 'metric' and 'non-metric' in preference to their rather longer synonyms.

A more precise classification is between 'nominal', 'ordinal', 'interval' and 'ratio' data. This is based on how much information the data contains. Nominal data is the most basic form of data, consisting of nothing more than names of categories, eg Gender is female or male. Ordinal data consists of categories that can be put in order, eg ranks in an army. Interval data is based on a scale of measurement that has consistent units between adjacent values, eg a price index such as the UK Consumer Price Index. Ratio data is, like interval data, based on a scale of measurement with consistent units but the difference is that the value of zero on the scale has meaning that is profound rather than arbitrary. Examples of ratio data include distance and time.

The type of data we have affects the choices we have for analysing it. In general the simpler the form of the data, the less choice there is. Analysis of nominal data is based on how frequently each category occurs. Ordinal data can be organized in this way but analysis of it can also be based on ranking. The numerical consistency of interval and ratio data permit a greater choice of analytical methods, including those based on arithmetical operations.

Data can be obtained from published or organizational sources. This is 'secondary data'; it has already been collected by others. Data that you collect yourself is 'primary data'. You might get it by direct measurement, eg timing how long it takes individuals to perform a task, or by asking individuals about themselves and their opinions using a standard approach such as a questionnaire.

Tell me more about data

Data is the plural form of datum, which means 'something that is given'. It is derived from the Latin verb *dare*, to give. The rules of English grammar suggest that as a plural noun we should say 'these data' and 'the data were collected'. Nowadays this is often ignored and data is treated as a singular noun so we say 'this data' and 'the data was collected' instead. Schagen (2007) explains why this is.

Data can take a number of forms depending on the nature of the variable we want to study. 'Variable' is a general term for a feature of interest. Examples of variables that we may want to study are Gender and Income; they vary between individuals. Each individual will have his or her own gender, which can be observed. The genders of individuals are 'observed values' or 'observations' of the variable Gender. Here I use Gender with a capital G for the variable and gender with a small g for individual values of the variable Gender. This reflects the convention in statistics of using capital letters, eg X and Y for variables, and lower case letters, eg x and y, for observations of those variables.

The basic distinction is between data that can be sorted by category, such as genders of individuals, and data that can be measured on a scale, such as income of individuals. Variables like Gender are categorical variables that have category values, in this case female and male. Variables like Income are measurement variables. Income has values measured in units of money. Note that although an individual's income is measured rather than observed in the way that an individual's gender can literally be observed, the terms 'observed value' and 'observation' are used for measurement variables like Income as well as categorical variables like Gender.

Instead of 'measurement' and 'categorical', their shorter synonyms 'metric' and 'non-metric' are used in this book. Metric means measurement, so metric data is based on measuring on a scale. The other basic type of data, categorical, is not based on measurement so it is non-metric. Common synonyms for measurement and categorical are 'quantitative' and 'qualitative'. Quantitative data is based on measuring or quantifying something on the scale of measurement for the variable, while with qualitative data the categories of the variable are qualitatively distinct. Distinguishing between metric and non-metric variables is important. Metric variables consist of observations using measurement, which are metric data. Non-metric variables consist of observations using categories, which are non-metric data.

Sometimes it is useful to apply the more elaborate NOIR classification model, which has four data types: nominal, ordinal, interval and ratio. Nominal and ordinal data are non-metric. Interval and ratio data are metric. The four data types differ in the amount of information they contain. Another way of putting this is that they have different levels of meaning. Since the point of statistical analysis is to get information from data, the more information the data contains, the more scope there is for using statistical analysis.

Of the four data types in the NOIR model nominal is the most primitive. The word 'nominal' means about names: this is all that nominal data is, just names or labels. The variable Gender is nominal; the names given to the observations are female and male. They are distinct categories with no systematic difference in importance or rank. There is no numerical connection between the two categories; one female does not equate to two males in the way that £100 equates to two £50s. Nominal data consists of names or labels but these may not be words. A telephone number is a number but it has no numerical value. It is just a label made up of numbers.

Ordinal data is based on order or rank within a defined structure. An example of ordinal data is the star rating awarded to hotels to reflect the quality and range of services they provide. The number of stars is a label or name attached to the hotel, but it is more than just a name; it places the hotel within the star ranking system. The more stars, the better the hotel: a two-star hotel is better than a one-star hotel, a three-star hotel better than a two-star hotel and so on. Although the stars allow hotels to be compared there is no systematic numerical basis for this. The stars used to rank hotels are points on a scale but these points are not measured in consistent units. There is no universal agreement on what a star means. In contrast there is agreement on what a metre or a degree Celsius means. This is the difference between ordinal and the higher forms of data, interval and ratio. We know that a four-star hotel should be better than a two-star hotel but does double the number of stars mean twice the quality in the same way as two kilometres is twice the distance of one kilometre? The answer is no, and this is the difference between ordinal and ratio data.

Measuring temperature provides a useful way of illustrating the difference between the two metric data types in the NOIR model, interval and ratio. In most of the world the Celsius (C) scale is used but the United States uses the Fahrenheit (F) scale. The key reference points on the Celsius scale are the freezing and boiling points of water, 0 °C and 100 °C. The equivalent points on the Fahrenheit scale are –32 °F and 212 °F. Why, you might ask, did Gabriel Fahrenheit use such odd reference points? The truth is they weren't odd to him. It is believed that when he was calibrating the thermometers he invented back in the early 18th century he set 0 °F at the coldest outside temperature he could find and 100 °F at his own body temperature.

The Celsius and Fahrenheit scales each have consistent units of measurement but do they measure heat consistently? Is 20 °C twice as hot as 10 °C? Convert these into Fahrenheit (68 °F and 50 °F) and the ratio between the two changes. This feature makes Celsius and Fahrenheit temperatures interval data not ratio data. Other examples of interval data are the values of stock exchange indexes such as the FTSE100, the Dow Jones and the Nikkei.

Ratio data has a logical rather than arbitrary zero and consistent ratios across different scales of measurement. The zero points in the Celsius and Fahrenheit scales may be logical but they were chosen. Compare this with weight. Zero kilograms and zero pounds mean the same: no weight. Four kilograms are twice two kilograms and the Imperial equivalent of four kilograms (8.8 lb) is twice the equivalent of two kilograms (4.4 lb).

Generally the differences between nominal and ordinal and between interval and ratio are less important than the difference between metric and non-metric. This is the key distinction to keep in mind when deciding what techniques you apply to the data you want to analyse. Statistical analysis enables you to give meaning to data; to change it into information, something that informs. To do this you have to use techniques that are appropriate for the type of data you have. Use the wrong technique and the results are of no use.

Telephone numbers are nominal data and non-metric. They are numbers, so we could work out the average of a set of telephone numbers. We could add up all the numbers and divide by how many we have. This would give us the average, known as the 'mean'. Because the numbers don't actually measure anything the average doesn't tell us anything. Working out the average is no more use than putting your shoes on your head. In contrast, working out the mean of a set of incomes is appropriate. Incomes are ratio data and metric, and things like average pay are widely used and understood.

Nominal data often consists of words rather than numbers. For non-metric, nominal variables like gender where the observed values are words, using arithmetic to work out an average is simply not possible. The general rule is that you should not use techniques that involve applying arithmetic to data unless it is metric data, ie interval or ratio data. Does this mean that if you have nominal or ordinal data, non-metric data, you cannot analyse it? No, it just means you should use other techniques. To analyse nominal data you can use proportions. To analyse ordinal data you can use not only proportions but also order statistics such as medians and quartiles.

When planning your project you need to consider how to get your data. You might want to collect it yourself; this would be primary data. You might get this by directly measuring or observing the things or people that are the subjects of your investigation. A good deal of scientific data is generated like this, such as weighing babies or testing the exhaust gases of cars. In business, research questionnaires are widely used to obtain primary data about the attitudes and behaviours of individuals, for instance their consumption patterns. If you do collect primary data you must ensure that however you do it, you collect observations of the variables you need to address your research questions. If one of your research questions is about the relationship between age and internet shopping you have to ask respondents their age as well as about their shopping habits.

Secondary data is data that is already available. You don't have to collect it yourself but you should find out as much as you can about how it was collected. This will help you ascertain how useful it is for your project. There are many sources of secondary data. Governments collect a vast amount of data and much of it is publicly available. The UK government provides a wide range of demographic and economic data on its **www.statistics.gov.uk** website. Organizations generate large amounts of data in the course of their business, for example sales, stocks and HR data which they publish in their company accounts.

Populations and samples

The essentials of populations and samples

When people use the word 'population' we generally assume they mean a human population, perhaps of a city, a country or the whole world. In statistics the word has a much broader meaning. The human population of a country is the total number of people who live there. For statisticians the notion of total is the key concept in their use of the word population. A population for them is not necessarily a human one, or indeed an animal one. It could be, but it could also be the total number of inanimate objects or incidences. A population could be all the cars in a city or all the transactions in a shop.

A sample is part of a population, usually a small part. A doctor may ask you for a blood sample. The point of a blood sample is to find out about all the blood in your body. In statistical analysis a sample has the same purpose. It helps us find out about the population it came from. The doctor has to rely on a sample of blood because taking all your blood would kill you; there is no choice for the doctor. For statistical analysis we could study an entire population or just a sample from it.

If we look at the population we get the whole picture, so why would we choose a sample? Most populations are large, which makes them expensive and time-consuming to study. Samples are a quicker alternative. The downside is that in using a sample to understand a population we are taking a chance that the sample represents the population. If samples are random, taken from a population in a way that every possible sample has the same chance of being selected, we can have a clear idea of the risks involved in sampling. If they are not taken at random we cannot. Non-random samples can give us some insight into the population but not on the same scientific basis as random samples.

Tell me more about populations and samples

In statistical analysis it is important to have a definition of exactly what or who is being investigated. A key preliminary stage is to be clear about the population, the complete set of whatever is being studied. They may be animate, ie people or animals, or inanimate, eg objects such as computers or events such as visits to a website. Each individual part of a population is called an 'element' of the population.

Populations can be large, eg all the cars produced by a company in a year, and sometimes so large that they are effectively infinite, eg the number of posts on a social network. Some populations are small, eg the number of directors in a company. If the population is small it is usually practicable to study the whole population. Studying the whole population is obviously the best way of understanding a population because you look at the lot; you don't miss anything out.

If the population is large studying all of it is unlikely to be practicable. In this case the only option is to take a sample from the population and study the sample. This will cost far less in both time and money. It also means that we don't have to track down all elements in the population. This is important if some are difficult or impossible to access. Many universities try very hard to find out what their students do after they graduate, which is very difficult if former students are working abroad and impossible if, as in fortunately very few cases, a former student has died.

Sampling makes it possible to find out about the population without studying all of it. For this to work it is important to take into account how the sample was taken from the population. If samples are drawn from the population on a random basis the sample results can be used to describe the population with an assessable degree of risk. Because a sample is always only part of the population we can never be certain it provides an accurate picture of the population; there is a risk that it will not. If you can measure this risk you can take it into account when reporting your findings.

Measuring risk

The essentials of measuring risk

There is a branch of mathematics called 'probability', which is about measuring risk. It is a substantial subject and most of it is outside the scope of this book. The importance of probability for statistical analysis is that it enables us to express succinctly the risks involved in using sample data to make judgements about the population the sample is from.

Probability measures risk on a scale that starts at 0 and finishes at 1. The extremes represent impossibility and certainty respectively. If the probability of something happening is 0 it cannot happen; if it is near 0 it is very unlikely. If it is 1 it is certain to happen; if it is near 1 it is very likely. If it is 0.5 it is as likely to happen as not to happen. This is what a 50/50 chance means.

How do we assess the probability of something happening? One way is to look at the mechanics of the process and reason it out. This is how we can work out the chance of getting a head on the toss of a coin. Another way is to repeat the process and count the number of times we get a head. This is the relative frequency approach. Sampling is a repeatable process; we could get many samples from a population. The use of probability in statistical analysis is based on relative frequency.

Tell me more about measuring risk

Probability started as a method the mathematicians Fermat and Pascal devised to analyse chance in gambling. Today probability is commonplace. It is used in, among other things, weather forecasting and insurance as well as gambling.

Probabilities can be given as percentages. This is often the case in statistics. A probability of 95 per cent means 19 times out of 20, which we can also express as 0.95. In statistical analysis probability is used to assess and communicate the results from analysing a random sample when these are used to describe a population. The terms 'confidence', 'p-value' and 'significance' are used in statistics to convey how much faith we can have in using sample results to draw conclusions about populations. They are all expressed as probabilities.

The many random samples we could get from a population will vary; they are not clones. If we know that the relative frequency of random samples having a feature in common is 0.95, or 95 per cent then we can say that we have 95 per cent confidence that the population has this feature.

How do we know that a certain proportion or relative frequency of samples will have something in common? For this we need to explore probability distributions. These map out the ways in which variables vary using probability.

The normal distribution and sampling distributions

The essentials of the normal distribution and sampling distributions

Probability distributions are models used to represent patterns of variations of variables. They show the way that all the observed values of all the elements in the population are distributed across the range of values of the variable. It is very rare that all the observed values of a whole population are available, especially if the population is large, so probability distributions are used as conceptual models of populations.

These distributions are general models that apply to different types of variable. Because they are general models they are not based on the frequencies of values of any one variable; instead they are based on probability. Just as gold can be exchanged into any currency, probabilities can be used to represent relative frequencies of values of any variable.

There are many probability distributions. We will concentrate on one, the normal distribution. This is an important distribution because it is the basis of the sampling distributions that map variation in sample results. The normal distribution is shown in Figure 1.1.

FIGURE 1.1   The normal distribution

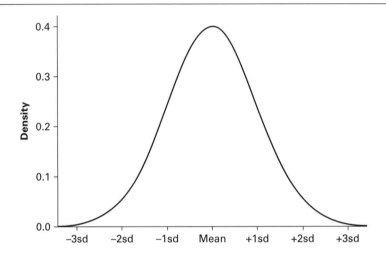

The scale on the horizontal axis in Figure 1.1 does not refer to one specific variable so it is marked out in general terms. At the centre of the distribution is the mean of the population. Either side of this the scale is marked out in standard deviation (sd) units. Starting from the left we have –3sd, which is three standard deviations to the left, or 'below' the mean. Next is –2sd, two standard deviations below the mean and so on. Finally we have +3sd, three standard deviations to the right, or 'above' the mean.

The scale on the vertical axis, Density, conveys how densely the values are packed along the distribution. The higher the line of the graph the more values are piled up. The line is not very high above –2sd on the horizontal axis so there are relatively few values around two standard deviations below the mean. The line is at its peak above the mean so there are relatively many values around there. The word 'relatively' is significant here. Because this is a general model distribution we use the general notion of relative frequency to define the density of values.

The normal distribution is a model for metric variables, those whose values are based on measurement on a scale. More specifically it models those variables that exhibit the normal pattern of variation. This pattern is symmetrical with the mean at the centre and the distribution tailing off to both left and right. Variables that have these features occur in human biology, agriculture, manufacturing processes and the measurement of human performance.

The standard 'bell' shape and use of standard deviations to mark out the horizontal scale make it possible to generalize about all variables that are normally distributed. Approximately two-thirds of the distribution lies within one standard deviation of the mean, about 95 per cent is within two standard deviations of it and almost the entire distribution within three.

It is worth knowing about the normal distribution because it is the root of sampling distributions. Samples are often the only way of investigating a population. The trouble is that samples are not all the same. We can draw a very large number of different samples from a population, even if we restrict our sampling to samples with a specific number of elements. Different samples will yield different results and the problem is that because sample results vary they can tell us different things about the population. We might want to know the mean of our population but the samples we could take will have different means. If we have some idea of how sample results vary we can anticipate the chances of any one mean giving us a good idea of the value of the population mean.

Sampling distributions show the variation in sample results. They are narrower and taller than the population distribution. Figure 1.2 shows a normal population distribution, the solid line, with the sampling distribution of means of all the random samples that consist of 25 elements that could be taken from the population, the broken line. The means of all samples of a given size will be distributed around the population mean. The population mean is at the centre of the distribution. The tighter spread around the mean is reflected in sampling distributions having smaller standard deviations.

FIGURE 1.2 The normal distribution (solid line) with the sampling distribution for n = 25

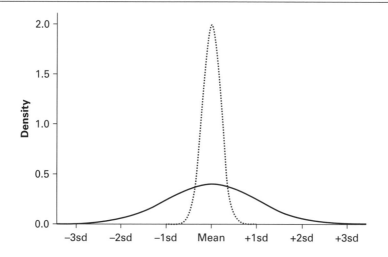

The standard deviation of a sampling distribution is known as the 'standard error'. The standard error of a sampling distribution is related to the standard deviation of the population the samples come from. The precise connection is that the standard error is the population standard deviation divided by the square root of the size of the samples. In Figure 1.3 the standard error is one-fifth of the population standard deviation.

One reason we take samples is if the population is very large. The other reason is that there is far less variation in sample results than in individual observations. This means that we have a much greater chance of getting an accurate estimate of something about the population from a sample than from an individual value.

Means of random samples taken from a normal population always form a sampling distribution that is normal in shape. Means of random samples taken from populations that do not have a normal shape also form a normal sampling distribution but only if the sample size is 30 or more, although approximately the case for sample sizes above 20.

To explain sampling distributions I have used sample means. These are used to estimate population means. This is not the only reason for looking at sampling distributions: other sample results belong to sampling distributions, including the results of many of the techniques covered in later chapters.

Tell me more about the normal distribution and sampling distributions

The normal distribution has two parameters, or key characteristics. The first is the mean, the average that is worked out by adding all the observations in the distribution and dividing by the number of observations. The mean tells us where the centre of the distribution is located. The parameter that tells us how widely dispersed the observations are around the centre is the standard deviation. This is based on the difference, or deviation of each observation from the mean. The larger the standard deviation the more spread out the observations are. Calculating the mean and the standard deviation involves arithmetic. This makes the normal distribution an appropriate model for metric variables, variables whose observations are metric data.

The normal distribution is a probability distribution. It maps out how likely the different values are to occur. Since the maximum value of a probability is 1, the total area inside the curve of the distribution is 1. Sections within the total area between points on the horizontal axis tell us the probability of the values between the points occurring. The mean is in the middle of the distribution. The probability of a value between the mean and the extreme left of the distribution is 0.5 or 50 per cent since half the total area is to the left of the mean. Approximately 95 per cent of the area is between the point two standard deviations to the left of the mean and the point two standard deviations to the right of the mean. The probability of a value between these points occurring is therefore 0.95 or 95 per cent.

The density scale on the vertical axis is engineered so that the total area is 1. In Figure 1.3 the density of the sampling distribution peaks much higher than the normal distribution because it is far narrower. The area within both distributions is 1.

The normal distribution is important because sampling distributions are often normal in shape. Sampling distributions are maps of results from random samples.

They are necessary because of the sheer number of different random samples we could take from a population, even if the population is quite small. Suppose I want to take a random sample of six students from a seminar of 18 students. There are 13,366,080 possible samples I could take. This number increases dramatically if I want to take a sample of six from the 150 students on the course. The number of different samples of six from the student population of the university (about 25,000) is so large it is in effect infinite.

FIGURE 1.3   The normal distribution (solid line) with the sampling distribution for n = 100

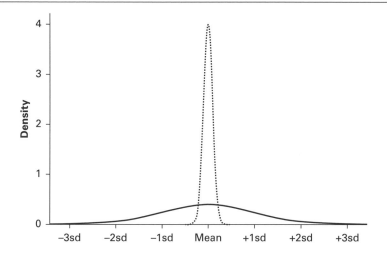

As Figure 1.2 shows, sampling distributions are taller and thinner than population distributions. The larger the sample size the more this is the case. The broken line in Figure 1.3 represents the sampling distribution for samples of 100 elements. The symbol for sample size is n, so in this case n = 100. In both Figure 1.2 and Figure 1.3 the population distribution seems to peak much lower than in Figure 1.1. It is the same distribution in each of the three diagrams. The difference is that the vertical scales in Figures 1.2 and 1.3 extend much further to accommodate the peaks of the sampling distributions.

To estimate the value of the mean of a large population it is better to use the mean of a random sample from the population than just a single observation from it. Look carefully at Figure 1.2: a far greater proportion of the sampling distribution (the broken line) than the population distribution (the solid line) is close to the population mean. This is even more so for the sampling distribution in Figure 1.3.

Every random sample taken from a population will have a mix of observations, some large, some small; calculating the sample mean balances out the large and the small. This is what is known as 'averaging out' and explains why sampling distributions are more concentrated than the distribution of the population from which the samples come, the 'parent' population that spawns the samples.

The larger the sample size, the more the averaging out and hence the more concentrated the distribution. The upshot is that not only is it better to use the mean of a sample than an individual observation to estimate the population mean, it is better to use the mean of a larger random sample than a smaller one. The disadvantage of using larger samples is that they almost always cost more to collect. Statistical analysis often involves balancing the desirable precision a large sample provides against the time and money incurred in gathering the data.

Analysing univariate data

02

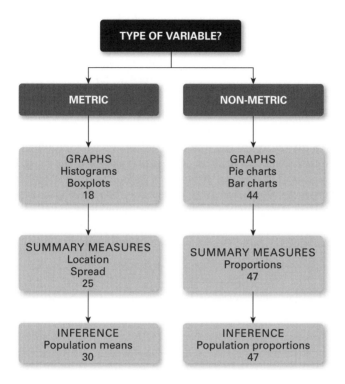

TYPE OF VARIABLE?

METRIC

NON-METRIC

GRAPHS
Histograms
Boxplots
18

GRAPHS
Pie charts
Bar charts
44

SUMMARY MEASURES
Location
Spread
25

SUMMARY MEASURES
Proportions
47

INFERENCE
Population means
30

INFERENCE
Population proportions
47

Topics in this chapter:

- Constructing histograms and boxplots to portray metric data.

- Measures of location and spread for metric data.

- Using sample means to estimate population means and test hypotheses about them.

- Compiling pie charts and bar charts to portray non-metric data.

- Using sample proportions to estimate population proportions and test hypotheses about them.

Histograms and boxplots

The essentials of histograms and boxplots

Histograms are also known as 'block diagrams'. They portray metric data that has been organized into classes. These classes are subsections of the measurement scale. They are also known as 'bins'. Together the classes cover the range of the set of observations, from the lowest to the highest.

Each class is represented in the diagram as a block. The size of the blocks depends on the number of observations in the classes they represent. The more frequent the observations, the larger the area of the block.

Drawing histograms used to begin with sorting the observations into classes to produce a grouped frequency distribution. Today specialist software such as Minitab or SPSS will generate a histogram directly from your data. In doing this the software sorts the observations into classes for you. It is possible to amend the classes if you are not happy with ones the software automatically sets.

Figure 2.1 is a histogram of the numbers of visitors to a sample of 68 city centre shops in one month. The measurement scale is plotted along the horizontal axis, also known as the x axis. The vertical axis, the y axis, has the scale of frequency. The number of visitors to shops, what is called the 'footfall', is a key performance measure for retailers. The diagram shows us that the majority of shops have footfalls between 85,000 and 105,000 with relatively few observations outside that range. There is one particularly large observation represented by the small block furthest on the right.

FIGURE 2.1 Histogram of the monthly footfall at 68 shops

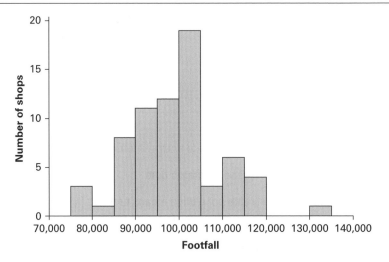

An alternative way of displaying distributions of metric data is the boxplot. The measurement scale is on the y axis; there is no measurement scale along the x axis.

Figure 2.2 is a boxplot of the same footfall data presented in the form of a histogram in Figure 2.1. The shape in Figure 2.2 is plotted using the five-point summary of the distribution. This consists of the minimum, the lower quartile, the median, the upper quartile and the maximum.

The shape in Figure 2.2 includes a horizontal line with a black dot on it. The position of this line in relation to the y axis is the median, approximately 100,000. The horizontal line below this median line marks the position of the lower quartile, approximately 90,000. The lowest point on the vertical line below the lower quartile line marks the position of the minimum observation, approximately 78,000.

FIGURE 2.2   Boxplot of the monthly footfall at 68 shops

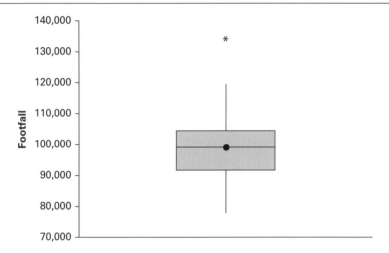

Above the median line in Figure 2.2 is another horizontal line. This marks the position of the upper quartile, approximately 105,000. The top of the vertical line above the upper quartile line marks the position of the maximum, approximately 120,000. In this case the top of the line marks the position of not the largest but the second largest observation. This is because there is a high outlier, represented by the asterisk above the top of the line. The value of the outlier is marked by the position of the asterisk against the vertical axis. It is approximately 133,000.

Histograms and boxplots are used to explore the nature of distributions, and specifically whether a distribution is symmetrical or skewed. Figure 2.1 indicates that the footfall distribution is approximately symmetrical, with similar tails to the left and right of the centre. Skewed distributions have longer tails on one side than on the other. The symmetry of the distribution is evident in Figure 2.2. The median line is about midway between the lower quartile line and the upper quartile line and the vertical lines above and below the central box are almost equal in length. Boxplots are particularly useful for comparing distributions. Both boxplots and histograms are used for initial investigation of metric data before applying more sophisticated techniques to it.

Tell me more about histograms and boxplots

To produce the histogram in Figure 2.1 the software I used, Minitab, sorted the data into classes for me. I simply typed in the observations (103,068, 87,990, 117,047 etc) then asked for a histogram. The software is programmed to set up classes and count how many observations fall into each class. The classes used to produce Figure 2.1 were:

70,000 and under 75,000
75,000 and under 80,000,
up to:

135,000 and under 140,000

In such software it is possible to specify the classes you want. Figure 2.3 portrays the same data as Figure 2.1, based on fewer but larger classes. The result is rather less detail. This may be adequate if you only need an outline of the distribution and is more appropriate if the number of observations in the distribution is small.

FIGURE 2.3   Histogram of the monthly footfall at 68 shops based on larger classes

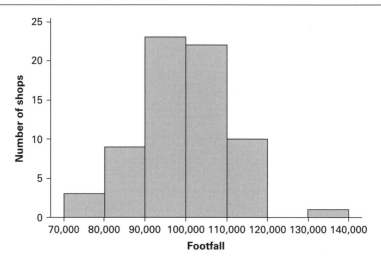

The histogram in Figure 2.4 portrays the same data as Figures 2.1 and 2.3 based on more but smaller classes. The result gives more detail and is better if there is a large number of observations in the distribution. As a rough guide the number of classes should be approximately the square root of the number of observations. For the footfall data the number of classes should be about the square root of 68, roughly 8 or 9. This is not an absolute rule. It is also important to make sure the classes start with round numbers. This makes it easier to use the histogram when discussing the distribution.

Boxplots are based on order statistics, which are used to construct the box at the heart of the diagram and the lines above and below it. Order statistics mark

FIGURE 2.4 Histogram of the monthly footfall at 68 shops based on more but smaller classes

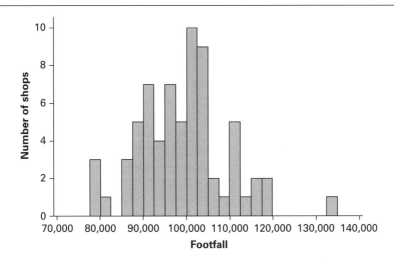

out the sequence of observations in order of magnitude. The minimum, the smallest observation, is represented by the lowest point of the vertical line below the box. The line between this point and the bottom of the box represents the lowest quarter of the observations. At the bottom of the box is the lower quartile line. The lower quartile is the point in the distribution above the quarter of observations that are the smallest in the distribution and below the remaining three-quarters of observations, all of which are larger than the lower quartile. It may help you to understand boxplots if you remember that the words 'quartile' and 'quarter' have the same root.

The lower part of the box, between the lower quartile line and the median line represents the second quarter of observations. These have values larger than the lower quartile but smaller than the median. The median is the half-way point in the distribution. Half of the observations are smaller than the median and half are larger.

The upper part of the box, between the median line and the upper quartile line at the top of the box, represents the quarter of observations that are larger than the median but smaller than the upper quartile. The upper quartile is the point in the distribution that separates the largest quarter of observations from the lower three-quarters. The vertical line above the box represents the largest quarter of observations.

A boxplot shows a distribution divided into four sections. These sections each contain a quarter of the observations. In Figure 2.2 each section contains a quarter of the observations, one-fourth of 68, ie 17. If you look carefully at Figure 2.2 you will see that the upper section of the box is smaller than the lower section. This does not mean that there are fewer observations represented by the upper section. Each section represents the same number of observations, 17. The difference in size between the sections reflects the fact that the 17 observations between the lower quartile and the median are more spread out than the 17 observations between the median and the upper quartile.

The asterisk in Figure 2.2 represents the one outlier in the distribution, the observation of about 133,000. Outliers are observations that are located some way away from the rest. They may arise as a result of measurement or recording error. This should be checked. If there is no error they should be investigated to find out what makes them so unusual. The outlier in Figure 2.2 may for instance be the footfall of a shop selling a heavily promoted item such as a new personal entertainment product.

Boxplots are particularly useful for comparing distributions. Two or more can be plotted in a single diagram. Figure 2.5 contains two plots. On the left is the footfall data plotted in Figure 2.2 and on the right monthly footfall data from the same shops five years earlier. Figure 2.5 shows that in general the footfall was higher five years ago. The median, represented in each plot by the horizontal line with a black dot, was higher five years ago. The upper quartile line in the plot on the left is at approximately the same height as the lower quartile line in the plot on the right. This means that only one quarter of the current footfalls is as high as three-quarters of the footfalls five years ago.

FIGURE 2.5   Comparative boxplot of monthly footfall: current and five years ago

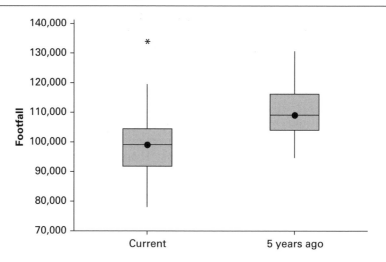

The shapes of histograms and boxplots are used to establish whether distributions are symmetrical or skewed. Skewed distributions have a concentration of observations to one side. If this concentration is to the left the distribution has a positive skew. The skew is called 'positive' because the long tail is on the right, towards the positive end of the numerical scale, which runs from minus infinity to plus infinity.

An example of positive skew is the distribution of a sample of music downloads shown in Figure 2.6. The diagram shows that the majority of songs are downloaded a relatively few times, 120 or less. There are a small number of tracks that were downloaded more frequently than this. These are the better selling tracks represented by the smaller blocks to the right.

FIGURE 2.6   Histogram of the numbers of downloads of 45 songs

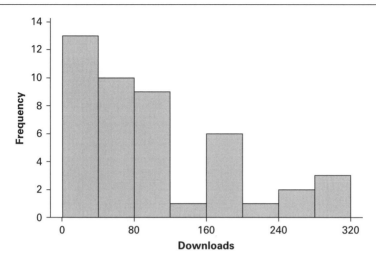

The boxplot in Figure 2.7 shows the same distribution of downloads as Figure 2.6. The skew in the distribution has resulted in the minimum, lower quartile and median being closer together than the median, upper quartile and maximum. The lower half of the distribution has considerably less spread than the upper half. There are no asterisks in the diagram, which implies there are no outliers in this distribution.

FIGURE 2.7   Boxplot of the numbers of downloads of 45 songs

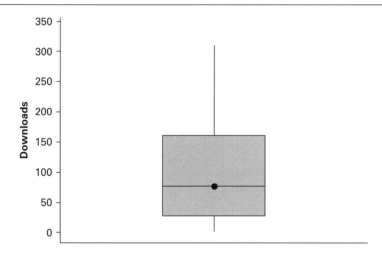

Skewed distributions with a concentration of observations to the right are 'negative' skewed. The long tail is on the left, towards the negative end of the numerical scale. Figure 2.8 is a histogram of the preparation times of a sample of 50 'three-minute

breakfasts' at a US diner. The larger blocks on the right show that the majority of observations are 165 seconds or more. The smaller blocks on the left indicate that faster preparation times are less common.

FIGURE 2.8   Histogram of preparation times of 50 breakfasts

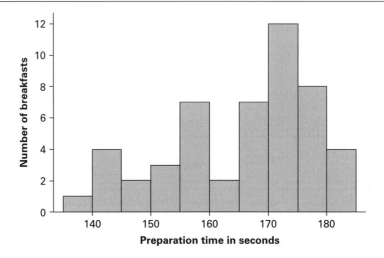

The boxplot in Figure 2.9 shows the same breakfast preparation times distribution as Figure 2.8. The negative skew distribution means the maximum, upper quartile and median are closer together than the median, lower quartile and minimum. The observations in the lower half of the distribution are more spread out than the observations in the upper half.

FIGURE 2.9   Boxplot of preparation times of 50 breakfasts

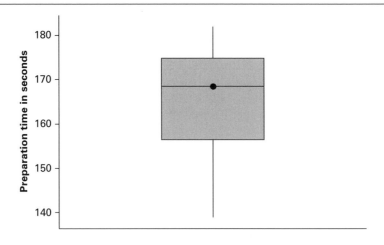

Measures of location and spread

The essentials of measures of location and spread

A histogram shows the overall shape of a distribution. A boxplot shows the shape in a different way. The structure of a boxplot is built around the median. The median is a summary measure that summarizes a key feature of a distribution, the centre of it.

There are two types of summary measures: measures of location and measures of spread. Measures of location are more commonly known as 'averages'. Another name for them is 'measures of central tendency'. The three measures of location in general use are the mean, the median and the mode. They all indicate where the centre of a distribution is located, but in different ways.

The mean of a set of metric data is the sum of the observations divided by the number of observations. This process is represented by the expression $\Sigma x/n$. Σ, the Greek capital S, is shorthand for 'sum of', x represents an individual observation and n represents the number of observations. The mean of a sample is represented by $\bar{x}$, x-bar. The mean of a population is represented by the lower case Greek m, μ, generally spelt in English mju and pronounced 'myou'. The difference in symbols is important because $\bar{x}$ is used to estimate μ.

The median is an order statistic. To find it the observations are arranged from the lowest to the highest. The median is the middle value.

The third measure of location is the mode. It is the most frequently occurring value in a set of data. In some circumstances it can be a useful way of summarizing data but is not part of more sophisticated statistical analysis.

The position of measures of location in relation to each other is a guide to the symmetry or skewedness of distributions. If the mean and median are the same or close the distribution is symmetrical. If the mean is larger than the median the distribution is positively skewed. If the mean is smaller than the median the distribution is negatively skewed.

Measures of spread summarize how the observations in a distribution are spread out. They are also called 'measures of dispersion' as they indicate how dispersed or scattered the observations are. There are four main measures of spread, although one is derived from another. The most basic is the range, which is simply the difference between the highest and lowest observations.

The interquartile range (IQR) is the difference between the upper and lower quartiles. Since one quarter of the observations are higher than the upper quartile and one quarter are lower than the lower quartile the IQR is the range over which the middle half of observations are spread. The semi-interquartile range (SIQR) is half the IQR.

Both the range and IQR are each based on just two observations. The standard deviation (sd) is a measure of spread based on all the observations. This inclusiveness makes it more reliable. The deviations are those between the mean and each observation. Working out the standard deviation involves squaring the deviations, adding them up, dividing this sum by n − 1 and taking the square root of the result. The process is represented by the following expression:

$$\sqrt{[\Sigma(x - \bar{x})^2/(n - 1)]}$$

The sd of a sample is represented by s, that of a population by sigma (σ), the Greek lower-case s.

The variance is the square of the sd. It is important in statistical analysis as it measures the total variation in a set of data. The success of statistical modelling is assessed by how much of the total variation the model explains. For all measures of spread, the greater the value the more spread there is in the distribution. The smaller the value the less spread there is in the distribution.

Usually measures of spread are used in combination with measures of location to give an overall indication of the nature of a distribution. The IQR or SIQR are used with the median because the quartiles and the median are order statistics. The sd or variance are used with the mean as they are based on deviations from the mean.

Summary measures are widely used to compare distributions. We may for instance be interested in average pay in one industry compared to another.

Tell me more about measures of location and spread

Averages are called 'measures of location' because they indicate where distributions are located on the measurement scale. The mode, median and mean are based on different approaches to location: they are used to convey where the centre of the distribution is and to represent the distribution as a whole.

The mode is the simplest average. Sometimes the mode is the most realistic summary measure to use. To illustrate this I could say that I have more than the average number of arms. People tend to think of the mean as the average. The mean number of arms is slightly less than two because some unfortunate people have lost arms in accidents or been born without them. I have two arms so I can say I have more than the average. Of course the overwhelming majority of people have two arms. Another way of saying this is that the mode of the distribution of number of arms is two. The mode in this case is a better way of summarizing the distribution than the mean.

Finding the mode of a set of observations is straightforward. You only need a tally of the observations, a count of how many times each one occurs. The one that occurs most is the mode. What limits the usefulness of the mode as a summary measure is that there may be no mode. Each value may occur only once. There may be more than one mode. There could be two values that occur exactly the same number of times. The consequence of this inconsistency is that the mode has little general use in statistics.

The median is the halfway point in the distribution. Half the observations are below the median and half above. To find the median we need to know how many observations there are, n, and arrange them by their size. The figures below are the numbers of employees in a sample of 13 restaurants of a multinational fast food company arranged in order of magnitude:

18 18 19 20 21 21 22 23 23 24 24 26 27

The position of the median is (n + 1)/2, which in this case is (13 + 1)/2, 7. The median is the 7th observation in the sequence, 22.

If there were an even number of observations the median is the mean of the middle pair. Suppose there was another restaurant which had 36 employees. The array of observations would be:

18   18   19   20   21   21   22   23   23   24   24   26   27   36

There are now 14 observations so the position of the median is $(14 + 1)/2$, 7.5. The median is the mean of the 7th and 8th observations, 22.5.

Note that in these distributions there are four modes since the values 18, 21, 23 and 24 each occur twice. In such cases the mode is of no use. A measure of location should be one figure that summarizes a distribution, not a choice from several.

The mean is the sum of the observations divided by how many there are. The mean number of employees of the 13 restaurants is:

$(18 + 18 + 19 + 20 + 21 + 21 + 22 + 23 + 23 + 24 + 24 + 26 + 27)/13$
$= 286/13 = 22$

Since both mean and median are the same, 22, we can conclude that this distribution is symmetrical. The mean and median of the footfall data shown in Figure 2.1 are 99244 and 99111. These are close, which affirms that the distribution is symmetrical. In contrast the mean and median of the downloads data shown in Figure 2.6 are 100.5 and 76.9. The mean is the higher figure, which reflects the positive skew in the distribution. The mean and median of the preparation times data shown in Figure 2.8 are 165.03 seconds and 168.56. Here the median is the higher figure, which reflects the negative skew in the distribution.

Of the four main measures of spread, the range is the simplest. For the restaurant employees data the range covered by the 13 observations is 9 – the difference between the largest observation, 27 and the smallest, 18.

To work out the interquartile range (IQR) we need to find the lower and upper quartiles. We can do this by working out the position midway between the smallest observation and the median. This is the median position, 7 plus 1 divided by 2, which is 4. The lower quartile is the 4th from lowest observation, 20. The upper quartile is the 4th from highest observation, one of the two 24s. The IQR is the difference between the lower and upper quartiles, which in this case is the difference between 20 and 24 – 4. The semi-interquartile range (SIQR) is half this –2.

Finding a standard deviation (sd) involves more calculation and generally we would use software to work it out. To illustrate the procedure I'll show you the calculation of the sd of the employees in the 13 restaurants. To start with we need the mean, 22. From this we subtract each observation then square the result. This is shown in Table 2.1.

The next step is to add up the squared deviations. Before I do that you may wonder why we bother squaring the deviations. After all, wouldn't it be simpler just to add up the deviations? Yes it would. Let's try it. Add up the figures in the 'Deviation from the mean' column and you should get 0. There are both positive and negative deviations and they cancel each other out. The reason this happens is that the mean of the distribution is like the centre of gravity of an object. The centre of gravity has as much weight on one side of it as on the other. Similarly the mean has as much

TABLE 2.1 Calculation of the squared deviations of the number of employees in 13 restaurants

Observation (x)	Mean ($\bar{x}$)	Deviation from the mean (x − $\bar{x}$)	Squared deviation (x − $\bar{x}$)²
18	22	−4	16
18	22	−4	16
19	22	−3	9
20	22	−2	4
21	22	−1	1
21	22	−1	1
22	22	0	0
23	22	1	1
23	22	1	1
24	22	2	4
24	22	2	4
26	22	4	16
27	22	5	25

numerical 'weight' to one side as the other. The effect is that deviations from the mean will always sum to 0. If we square the deviations the results will always be positive so the cancelling out problem disappears.

The next step is to add up the squared deviations, which in this case gives us 98. We then divide this by 1 less than n, the number of observations. Why 1 less than n rather than just n? The answer is that if we want to use s, a sample sd to estimate σ, a population sd dividing by n − 1 to get the sample sd produces a more reliable estimate of σ than dividing by n. Since sample sds are often used as estimates of population sds, dividing by n − 1 is the normal way of working out the sample sd from the sum of the squared deviations. For the employees data we divide 98 by one less than 13, 12, which gives us 8.17 to two decimal places. Is this the sd? Not yet. In fact it is the square of the sd, the variance. To get the sd we have to take the square root of 8.17. This makes sense as we squared the deviations at

TABLE 2.2 Calculation of the squared deviations of the number of employees in 14 restaurants

Observation (x)	Mean ($\bar{x}$)	Deviation from the mean (x − $\bar{x}$)	Squared deviation (x − $\bar{x}$)^2
18	23	−5	25
18	23	−5	25
19	23	−4	16
20	23	−3	9
21	23	−2	4
21	23	−2	4
22	23	−1	1
23	23	0	0
23	23	0	0
24	23	1	1
24	23	1	1
26	23	3	9
27	23	4	16
36	23	13	169

an earlier stage. It also means that the sd is in the same units, employees, as the observations. The square root of 8.17 is 2.86 to two places of decimals, which is the sample sd.

The larger the sd, the more spread there is in the distribution. If there is another restaurant with 36 employees we would expect the sd to be more than 2.86 because the additional observation is larger than the others and increases the spread in the data. We can work out the sd of the 14 observations, starting with the calculations in Table 2.2.

Note that including the observation 36 has increased the value of the mean to 23. The sum of the squared deviations is 280. Dividing this by n − 1, which is now 13, produces 21.54. The square root of this is the sd, 4.64. This is considerably larger than the sd of 2.86 we calculated for the original 13 observations.

We can summarize the distribution of employees at the 13 restaurants by saying it has a median of 22 and an IQR of 4. Alternatively we could describe it as having a mean of 22 and a standard deviation of 2.86. By combining measures of location and spread in this way we can compare and contrast distributions. The footfall data shown in Figure 2.1 has a mean of 99,244 and a standard deviation of 10,344. The footfall data from five years earlier, portrayed in the plot on the right in Figure 2.5, has a mean of 109,670 and a standard deviation of 7,838. This demonstrates that the footfall five years ago was on average higher with less spread. The shops seemed to be attracting more visitors then and there was more consistency in visitor numbers.

Inference: estimation and hypothesis testing of population means

The essentials of estimation

To infer means to conclude, so inference is about drawing conclusions. Statistical inference is the use of sample data to find out about the population that the sample comes from. Since getting sample data is cheaper and quicker than surveying the whole population this is very useful. In a research project such as yours it is almost certain that you will only be able to generate sample data.

The samples we use for statistical inference should be random samples. This is because inference techniques are based on sampling distributions and sampling distributions model the patterns of variation among summary measures of *random* samples.

There are two types of statistical inference. The first is estimation. You work out a sample statistic, which is simply another name for a summary measure of a sample, and use this to estimate a population parameter. The case we look at in this section is using the sample mean to estimate the population mean. Other sample statistics are used in the same way, such as using the sample standard deviation to estimate the population standard deviation.

The second type of statistical inference is hypothesis testing. Estimation begins with the sample, while hypothesis testing begins with the population. The first step in estimation is to produce something from the sample data; the first step in hypothesis testing is to state something that is believed to be true about the population. This is the null hypothesis. We also specify the negation of this, the alternative hypothesis. This pair of hypotheses should together cover all possibilities. The next step is to use sample data to test the null hypothesis. The final stage is to state which of the hypotheses is the more credible.

In both types of statistical inference conclusions about populations are based on sample evidence. We can get very many different samples from a population and they will not be the same. This means that predictions and judgements about populations based on sample data are inevitably less than absolutely certain. To reflect this uncertainty probability is use to convey the rigour of the results of statistical inference.

Earlier in the chapter we used monthly footfall data from 68 shops. Let's assume that this is a random sample of city centre shops and we want to use it to estimate the mean monthly footfall of all city centre shops in the country. This is the population mean, μ, which we don't know because we don't have footfall data for all shops, the population. What we do know is that the sample mean $\bar{x}$ of our random sample of 68 shops is 99,244.

We could simply use the sample mean, 99,244, as an estimate of the population mean. This is an example of point estimation, the use of a statistic from a sample to estimate its population equivalent. This is of limited use because we don't know how viable the estimate is. To put it another way we don't know how confident we can be about the accuracy of the estimate.

Confidence in estimation is how often your estimate will be accurate if you repeated the process: 90% confidence means that 9 in every 10 estimates will be accurate, 95% that 19 out of 20 will be accurate and 99% that 99 out of 100 will be accurate. We can't gauge the confidence of a point estimate. How then can we estimate with a given level of confidence? The answer is to produce a confidence interval (CI). This is a range with the sample statistic in the middle. The width of the range, or interval, depends on two things: the spread of the sampling distribution and the level of confidence.

We can decide what level of confidence to use. There is an important trade-off involved in this. The higher the level of confidence the wider the interval *but* the wider the interval the less precise it is. There is another factor to consider. This is the sample size. Means of larger samples vary less than means of smaller samples. It follows that estimation based on larger samples is more consistent. With larger samples we can have either higher levels of confidence or greater precision, or indeed both.

So far we have said that confidence intervals are a better form of estimation than point estimates because we can have a good idea of the chances of being right. But how do we construct a confidence interval? In our example we start with the sample mean, 99,244. This will be at the centre of the confidence interval. To create the interval we add and subtract what is called the 'error', which consists of two components. One is the standard error, which is the standard deviation of the sampling distribution to which the sample statistic belongs. By using the standard error we take account of the variation inherent in sampling. The other component is the number of standard errors to be added and subtracted. This controls the level of confidence: the higher the level of confidence the more standard errors we need to add and subtract.

If the sample size is more than 30 the sampling distribution will definitely be normal in shape: 95% of the normal distribution is within approximately two standard deviations of the centre of the distribution. The more precise figure is 1.96, so if we take a sample mean and add and subtract 1.96 standard errors we create a 95% confidence interval.

The sample mean monthly footfall of the 68 shops is 99,244. The sample standard deviation is 10,344. From this we can estimate the standard error of the sampling distribution, which is the population standard deviation, σ, divided by the square root of the sample size, n. We don't know the population standard deviation so we can't work out the standard error, but using the sample standard deviation we can get an estimate for the standard error. This is $10,344/\sqrt{68}$, which is 1254.4 to one decimal place.

The 95% confidence interval (CI) for the population mean monthly footfall is 99,244 plus and minus 1.96 times the estimated standard error, 1254.4. The results:

$$99244 + (1.96 * 1254.4) = 101,702.6 \text{ and } 99244 - (1.96 * 1254.4) = 96,785.4$$

Our 95% confidence interval is, to the nearest whole number, 96,785 to 101,703. Based on our sample evidence we can be 95% confident that the population mean monthly footfall is somewhere between 96,785 people and 101,703 people. This does not mean that the population mean will definitely be within these two figures, but 95 times out of 100 it will be.

For a 99% level of confidence we need to add and subtract 2.58 standard errors. Why 2.58? This is because 99% of the normal distribution is within 2.58 standard deviations either side of the centre of the distribution. A 99% CI for the population mean monthly footfall works out as 96,008 (which is $99244 - 2.58 * 1254.4$) to 102,480 (which is $99244 + 2.58 * 1254.4$). This is wider than the 95% CI interval (96,785 to 101,703). We have sacrificed precision for a higher level of confidence.

Suppose instead of a sample of 68 we had a much bigger sample, 100, and had the same mean and standard deviation as the sample of 68. The estimated standard error would be $10,344/\sqrt{100}$ which is 1,034.4. The 99% confidence interval would be 96,580 (which is $99244 - 2.58 * 1034.4$) to 101,908 (which is $99244 + 2.58 * 1034.4$). This is narrower than the 99% CI based on the sample of 68 (96,008 to 102,480). The larger sample produces a more precise confidence interval.

The numbers of standard errors we have used in constructing confidence intervals, 1.96 for 95% and 2.58 for 99%, are points in the normal distribution. They are generic. Whatever the mean and the standard deviation of the normal distribution, 95% of the distribution is always between 1.96 standard deviations to the left of the mean and 1.96 standard deviations to the right of it. Similarly 99% of the distribution is always between 2.58 standard deviations to the left and to the right of the mean.

Before computers statisticians used what they called the 'standard' normal distribution as a benchmark for calibrating the normal distribution. This was also known as the 'z distribution' and the points such as 1.96 and 2.58 were referred to as 'z values'.

As long as the sample size is 30 or more the sampling distribution of sample means is normal in shape. But what if the sample size is less than 30? In this case the sampling distribution is roughly normal but only as long as the population distribution is normal. Unfortunately it is not sufficiently normal to allow us to use the same numbers of standard errors, the z values as we have done so far in constructing confidence intervals.

Sampling distributions of means of samples of less than 30 are more spread out than the normal distribution, and the smaller the sample size the more spread out are the sample means. Producing confidence intervals from small samples involves using a modified version of the normal distribution known as the 't distribution'. The t distribution is flatter than the normal distribution but has the same symmetry and central peak. I have called it the 't distribution' but in fact there are different versions of it; the one we use depends on the sample size. Specifically it is the number of degrees of freedom in the sample data, which is one less than the sample size.

For a confidence interval of the population mean number of employees in the fast food restaurants we have to use the t distribution as the sample size is only 13. For a 95% CI we can't use 1.96, the z value we used for the footfall data. Instead we use the value in the t distribution that is the number of standard deviations we would have to go to the left and right of the middle to encompass 95% of the distribution. This is 2.179, which is larger than 1.96. It comes from the t distribution that has 12 degrees of freedom, one less than the sample size, 13.

The 95% CI is the sample mean, 22 minus and plus 2.179 standard errors. The estimated standard error is the sample standard deviation, 2.86 divided by the square root of the sample size, 13 – 0.79 to two places of decimals. The results of this process, to two places of decimals are 20.27 (= 22 – 2.179 * 0.79) and 23.73 (= 22 + 2.179 * 0.79). We can be 95% confident that the population mean number of employees is between 20.27 and 23.73.

For a 99% CI we use the larger t value of 3.055. In a t distribution with 12 degrees of freedom, 99% is between 3.055 standard deviations to the left of the mean and 3.055 standard deviations to the right of the mean. The results are 19.58 (= 22 – 3.055 * 0.79) and 24.42 (= 22 + 3.055 * 0.79). We can be 99% confident that the population mean number of employees is between 19.58 and 24.42.

Tell me more about estimation

At first sight the process of statistical estimation can seem a bit like a conjuring trick. After all, how can we possibly say that we have a specific level of confidence in an estimate based on just one sample? If we have a 95% confidence interval how do we know that 19 times out of 20 it will be accurate?

To answer this let's return to the notion of the sampling distribution. This is basically a map of how the results from all the samples of a particular size vary. The mean of a sampling distribution of sample means is the population mean and the spread is measured by the standard error. For samples of 30 or more elements the sampling distribution of the mean is normal in shape. Normal distributions are calibrated in standard deviations, or in the case of sampling distributions, in standard errors.

The benchmark distribution we used in estimation with samples of 30 or more is the standard normal distribution aka the z distribution; this is shown in Figure 2.10. The shaded tails at either end are each 0.025 or 2.5% of the distribution and are marked off by the points –1.96 on the left and 1.96 on the right. The unshaded area between these tails is 0.95 or 95% of the distribution, which is the proportion of the distribution within 1.96 of the mean, 0. The standard deviation of the standard normal distribution is 1, so another way of putting this is that 95% of the distribution is within 1.96 standard deviations of the mean. This is true for the normal distribution whatever the value of the standard deviation, or, in the case of sampling distributions that are normal, the standard error.

FIGURE 2.10 The standard normal distribution

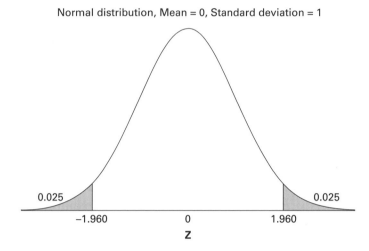

Normal distribution, Mean = 0, Standard deviation = 1

0.025   0.025

−1.960   0   1.960

Z

I'll use the US diner case to illustrate why a 95% confidence interval will be accurate 95% of the time. Let's pretend we know the mean and standard deviation of the 'three-minute breakfast': 160 and 12 seconds respectively. Suppose that we want to use a sample size of 36 to estimate the population mean preparation time. The sample means of all the possible samples consisting of 36 observations that could be taken will form a sampling distribution with a mean of 160 and a standard error of 2 (= $12/\sqrt{36}$). This is shown in Figure 2.11. As in Figure 2.10 the two 0.25 or 2.5% tails are marked off at 1.96 standard errors either side of the mean; on the left hand

FIGURE 2.11 The sampling distribution of sample mean preparation times (n = 36)

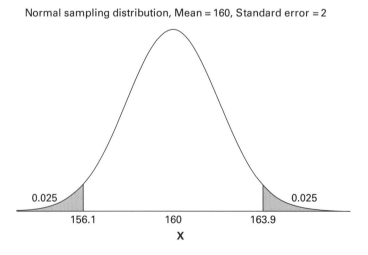

Normal sampling distribution, Mean = 160, Standard error = 2

0.025   0.025

156.1   160   163.9

X

side at 156.1 (= 160 − 1.96 * 2) and on the right at 163.9 (= 160 + 1.96 * 2). This demonstrates that 2.5% of all sample means from samples will be less than 156.1, 2.5% more than 163.9 and the remaining 95% between 156.1 and 163.1.

To obtain a 95% confidence interval from a sample of 30 or more we would take 1.96 standard errors away from the sample mean and add 1.96 standard errors to the sample mean. For the preparation times sampling distribution for sample size 36, 1.96 standard errors is 3.9 to one place of decimals.

Suppose we take some samples, each consisting of 36 observations. Let's say the first has a sample mean of 162. When we add and subtract 3.9 we create an interval of 159.1 (= 162 − 3.9) to 165.9 (= 162 + 3.9). Although the sample mean, 162, is higher than the population mean, of 160, the interval we created does contain the population mean within it. Imagine we take some more samples. The next one has a mean of 157.6. The 95% confidence interval based on this is 153.5 (= 157.6 − 3.9) to 160.5 (= 157.6 + 3.9). Again this does contain the population mean within it. Notice that both sample means so far are between 156.1 and 163.9, the points marking off the 2.5% tails in the sampling distribution. What happens if we have a sample mean outside this range, say 165.2? The interval from this is 161.3 (= 165.2 − 3.9) to 169.1 (= 165.2 + 3.9). This does not contain the population mean within it.

We could go on. Every time we have a sample mean between 156.9 and 163.9 the interval we create will contain the population mean. Every time we have one that is outside this range the interval will not contain the population mean. Since 95% of the sample means are between 156.9 and 163.9, 95% of samples will produce an interval that does contain the population mean. This is why we can describe them as 95% confidence intervals.

A question that often arises in the planning of a project involving estimation is how large the sample needs to be. If you know how precise you want your confidence interval to be, ie the maximum error, the confidence level you would like, and the population standard deviation, you can work out the necessary sample size, n. The formula for this is:

$$n = (z_{\alpha/2} * \sigma/error)^2$$

The z value has the suffix $\alpha/2$. This is half the proportion of estimates that you will allow to be wrong. Its job in the formula is to reflect the level of confidence. If this is 95%, or 0.95 then α is 0.05. Half of this is 0.025. The z value that cuts off a right-hand side tail of 0.025 is 1.96, as shown in Figure 2.10. This is $z_{\alpha/2}$ for a 95% confidence interval.

Suppose we want to estimate the population mean preparation time for the 'three-minute breakfasts' at the diner to within 2 seconds with 95% confidence. If the population standard deviation is 12 seconds the sample size required is:

$$n = (1.96 * 12/2)^2 = 138.3 \text{ to one decimal place}$$

Because a sample size must be a whole number we have to round this result, and we always round up to ensure that the maximum error is not exceeded. The required sample size is therefore 139. We do this even when numerically it seems more logical to round down, as in this case.

Perhaps 139 is too large a sample to collect. What sample size would be required if we relaxed our precision requirement to three seconds?

$$n = (1.96 * 12/3)^2 = 61.5 \text{ to one decimal place, so } 62$$

In practice we are unlikely to know the population standard deviation. Typically the figure used is an approximation based on a pilot study or published analysis of the topic.

When our estimates of population means are based on means of samples of less than 30 elements we use the t distribution. The t distribution is a bit more difficult to use than the z distribution. There is only one z distribution but different t distributions. The choice of t distribution depends on the degrees of freedom, which is the sample size minus 1. But what exactly are degrees of freedom and why do they matter? Let me answer the last part of the question first. They matter because in estimation we take the sample mean as fixed. If it is fixed we lose a degree of freedom in what the observations in the sample could be. Let me try to illustrate this. Suppose you are taking a flight with two friends and you each have one bag to check in and the airline has a rule that the mean weight of the bags of a group of passengers travelling together must not exceed 20 kg. Your friends have packed their bags and they weigh 22 kg and 20 kg. You want to take as much as you can but keep to the rule. Your bag cannot weigh more than 18 kg. How do I know? For the mean weight to be 20 kg the aggregate weight of the three bags must be 60 kg. Your friends have already used up 42 kg, leaving you with 18 kg. You have lost the freedom to choose any other weight because the sample mean is fixed.

The essentials of hypothesis testing

I think of hypothesis testing as estimation turned on its head. To estimate we use the sample data to find out about the population. To test a hypothesis we specify what we believe to be true about the population and use sample data to ascertain whether we are right.

Hypothesis testing starts with a null hypothesis. This is what we want to test. It is what we or perhaps others suggest the population is like. For the footfall data we may think the population mean monthly footfall in city centre shops is 100,000. The standard hypothesis testing notation is to use H for hypothesis. The null hypothesis is represented as H_0. Using this notation the null hypothesis for the footfall data is $H_0: \mu = 100,000$; 100,000 is the hypothesized population mean.

The alternative hypothesis is what must be true if the null hypothesis isn't. If the null hypothesis is that the population mean monthly footfall is 100,000 the alternative hypothesis is that it is not 100,000. The symbol for alternative hypothesis is H_1, so for the footfall example $H_1: \mu \neq 100,000$.

Now we have specified the hypotheses we must consider how to use the sample data to select which of the two hypotheses is the more credible. The sample of 68 shops had a mean monthly footfall of 99,244. This is less than 100,000, which suggests that the population mean is less than 100,000 and so we should reject the null hypothesis. But before we reach such a conclusion we have to consider the sampling distribution.

The question is not whether the sample mean is the same as the supposed value of the population mean or not. Relatively few sample means will be: the majority will be higher or lower. The key question is how much higher or lower. Does our sample mean differ so much from the supposed population mean that it is hard to believe that our sample came from a population with that mean? How do we judge this?

The answer is that we consider where the sample mean is in the sampling distribution that it belongs to. We don't know the actual population mean so we can't know the definite position of the sampling distribution. Remember that the mean of the sampling distribution is the population mean. To resolve this we assume that the null hypothesis is true until we have good reason to believe otherwise. It's a bit like the 'innocent until proved guilty' presumption in English law.

For the monthly footfall case the null hypothesis is that the population mean is 100,000. Assume this is true. All the possible samples of 68 that we could take from the population would have means that form a sampling distribution with a mean of 100,000. Our sample mean of 99,244 is 756 below the mean. This seems a lot, but is it a 'significant' difference; ie is the difference large enough to make us think the population mean is very unlikely to be 100,000? The greater the difference between the sample mean and the hypothesized population mean, the more likely we are to doubt the hypothesized population mean. In the footfall case our sample mean is 756 less than the hypothesized population mean, 100,000. This might cause us to doubt that the population mean really is 100,000, but what if our sample mean were 89,244? We would have more doubt that the population mean is 100,000; if the sample mean were 79,244, even more doubt.

The distance between the sample mean and the hypothesized population mean is only part of the story. We have to consider the spread in the sampling distribution. This is measured by the standard error. We can only work out the actual standard error if we know the population standard deviation. In the footfall case we don't know this so we will have to use the sample standard deviation as a proxy. The estimated standard error is 1254.4 (= $10,344/\sqrt{68}$). Knowing the estimated standard error allows us to locate the sample mean in the sampling distribution. With this we can assess how likely such a sample mean is to occur if the population mean is the one that the null hypothesis suggests.

The footfall sample mean of 99,244 is 756 less than 100,000, the hypothesized population mean. The number of estimated standard errors between 99,244 and 100,000 is 756/1254.4, 0.60 to two places of decimals. This is called the test statistic because it enables us to test the hypotheses.

So, our sample mean is 0.6 standard errors less than the hypothesized mean. How likely is such a sample mean? We can ascertain this by referring to the standard normal distribution. The probability that a value 0.6 or more standard deviations to the left of the mean occurs in a normal distribution is 0.2743. How do I know this? I typed =NORMDIST(–0.6,0,1,TRUE) in the formula bar in EXCEL. The entries in brackets are –0.6, the number of standard errors less than the mean, 0 and 1, the mean and standard deviation of the standard normal distribution, and TRUE to request a cumulative probability.

The result, 0.2743, suggests that there is a better than one in four chance of getting a sample mean of 99,244 or less if the population mean is 100,000. This is hardly a long shot so we would conclude that the null hypothesis is reasonable; the population mean could be 100,000. Note that it doesn't mean that the population mean is definitely 100,000 – we would have to survey the whole population to find the population mean.

I have just described the orthodox approach to hypothesis testing. Let me tell you about an alternative approach you may prefer that should help you interpret statistical software results more readily. Using EXCEL, or for that matter Minitab or SPSS, we can sidestep the standard normal distribution. In EXCEL we can type =NORMDIST(99244,100000,1254.4,TRUE) in the formula bar. The result, 0.2734 to four places of decimals, is more accurate than the 0.2743 as I rounded the test statistic to –0.6. In this alternative approach the result is known as the p value. It is the probability of getting the sample mean, or one further from the hypothesized population mean if the null hypothesis is true, in this case if the population mean is really 100,000. A p value is also interpreted, rather loosely, as the probability that the null hypothesis is true.

Suppose our sample mean footfall was 103,244 not 99,244. This is further from 100,000, being 3,244 higher. This suggests the real population mean is higher than 100,000. Again, before jumping to this conclusion we need the test statistic and consequent p value. The test statistic is 2.59 to two decimal places (3244/1254.4). The probability of this or a higher value is about half a per cent. To get this I used the formula =NORMDIST(103244,100000,1254.4,TRUE) in EXCEL. The result, 0.995 to three decimal places is the probability of a test statistic less than 2.59. I took this away from 1 to get the probability the test statistic is 2.59 or more. This probability of half a per cent suggests that if the null hypothesis is true and the population mean really is 100,000 we would expect a sample mean of 103,244 or higher only 1 in every 200 samples. This is very small. It is difficult to reconcile a sample mean of 103,244 with a population mean of 100,000. Unless we have good reason to question the sample result, perhaps on the basis of measurement or processing, it is logical to doubt the null hypothesis and reject it.

How low should the p value be before we reject the null hypothesis? The figure of 0.05 is probably the most widely used. This means that if the sample result is less likely than once in every 20 samples we should reject the null hypothesis. A more exacting standard is 0.01, which means rejecting the null hypothesis if the sample result is less likely to occur than once in every 100 samples. The threshold p value below which we would reject the null hypothesis is known as the 'level of significance'.

Going back to the footfall case, there is something important to note about the hypotheses. The null hypothesis, H_0, was that the population mean is 100,000. The alternative hypothesis, H_1, was that the population mean is not 100,000. This is an example of a two-sided alternative hypothesis: there are two ways of rejecting it, either because the sample mean is significantly lower than the hypothesized population mean or it is significantly higher. Because of the nature of the alternative hypothesis the p value is the probability of a sample mean being as far or further as our sample mean is from the hypothesized population mean on *either* one side *or* the other of the sampling distribution. The probabilities we used above are actually only half the story. The sample mean of 99,244 produced a test statistic of –0.6 and the probability of such a value or a lower one was 0.2743. The sampling distribution to which the sample mean belongs is normal in shape and hence symmetrical. This means that the probability of a sample result producing a test statistic of -0.6 or less, 0.2743, is exactly the same as the probability of the sample result producing a test statistic of 0.6 or more. The p value is the sum of these probabilities, twice 0.2743, which is 0.5486. This is the probability of getting a sample mean 756 or more below 100,000 or 756 or more above 100,000.

Two-sided tests are the default setting for hypothesis testing but there are contexts when a one-sided test is more appropriate. Consider the breakfast preparation times shown in Figures 2.8 and 2.9. Suppose we want to allow 20 seconds for breakfasts to be served to customers at their tables. If the diner claims to offer 'three-minute breakfasts' on average, the population mean preparation time would have to be 160 seconds. It doesn't matter if it is less but it does matter if it is more.

We can test the null hypothesis that the population mean preparation time is 160 seconds or less (H_0: $\mu \leq 160$) against the alternative hypothesis that it is more than 160 seconds (H_1: $\mu > 160$). This is a one-sided test. The sample mean is 165.03 and the sample standard deviation is 12.10. The test statistic is 2.94 to two decimal places; the difference between the sample mean and the hypothesized population mean, 5.03 ($= 165.03 - 160$) divided by the estimates standard error, 1.71 ($= 12.10/\sqrt{50}$). The probability that the test statistic is 2.94 or more is 0.002, which is the p value. This does not need to be doubled as it is a one-sided test. Our conclusion is that the null hypothesis should be rejected at the 1% level of significance. The population mean seems to be higher than 160 seconds. Here we reject the null hypothesis because the sample mean is significantly larger than the hypothesized population mean.

What if the samples are small, which in inference about the population mean is when they contain less than 30 elements? In such cases we use the t distribution not the z distribution as the benchmark for the sampling distributions; we conduct a t test and not a z test. The effect of this is to require a greater difference between the sample result and the hypothesized population parameter for the same level of significance.

To illustrate this let's revisit the data for the number of employees at the 13 restaurants listed in Table 2.1. The sample mean was 22 and the sample standard deviation 2.86. Suppose the restaurant chain claims that its restaurants have on average 24 employees. To assess the validity of the claim we can test the null hypothesis that the population mean is 24 (H_0: $\mu = 24$) against the alternative hypothesis that it is not 24 (H_1: $\mu \neq 24$). The test statistic, -2.52 to two decimal places is the difference between the sample mean and the hypothesized population mean, -2 ($= 22 - 24$) divided by the estimated standard error, 0.79 ($= 2.86/\sqrt{13}$) to two decimal places. The probability of a test statistic of -2.52 or less is 0.0135. To get this I used =T.DIST(-2.52,12,TRUE) in EXCEL. The 12 is the number of degrees of freedom, which is one less than the sample size, 13. Because this is a two-sided test the p value is twice 0.0135, 0.0270. This is less than the 0.05 threshold so we should reject the null hypothesis. As the sample mean of 22 is less than the hypothesized population mean of 24 we can conclude that the real population mean is likely to be lower than 24.

If instead of the t distribution we used the z distribution, what difference would it make? Using the equivalent formula in EXCEL, =NORMDIST(-2.52,0,1,TRUE) produces a probability of 0.006. Doubling this, as it is a two-sided test, gives a p value of 0.012. This is less than half of the p value of 0.0270 we obtained using the t distribution. As it is lower it suggests that the sample result is more significant than it really is. We should reject the null hypothesis but only on the basis of the t test.

Tell me more about hypothesis testing

There are five basic steps in hypothesis testing: specify the hypotheses, access the sample data, calculate the test statistic, find the p value, and draw the conclusion. The first of these sometimes causes problems. If you find this tricky you might find the guidance in Table 2.3 useful. The symbol μ_0 represents the hypothesized population mean.

TABLE 2.3   Combinations of hypotheses and decision criteria

Null hypothesis	Alternative hypothesis	Type of test	When to reject H_0
$H_0: \mu = \mu_0$	$H_1: \mu \neq \mu_0$	Two-sided	$\bar{x}$ significantly high or low
$H_0: \mu \leq \mu_0$	$H_1: \mu > \mu_0$	One-sided	$\bar{x}$ significantly high
$H_0: \mu \geq \mu_0$	$H_1: \mu < \mu_0$	One-sided	$\bar{x}$ significantly low

The tests we have looked at so far are used to probe possible values of population means. Another type of hypothesis testing is where we have two samples and want to ascertain if they come from the same population. There are basically two ways of doing this, depending on the whether the data we have is paired or not.

Often paired data consists of 'before' and 'after' measurements for the same sample of elements. The test is based on the differences between the two measurements for each individual element. To illustrate the technique, suppose we have monthly footfall data from 10 shops, now and five years ago. These figures are in the first and second columns of Table 2.4. The third column contains the results from subtracting the figure from five years ago from the figure now. These differences will be used to work out the test statistic.

The sample size is less than 30 so we use the t distribution to conduct a paired t test. Usually the null hypothesis in a paired t test is that the population mean difference, μ_d is 0. The population mean difference is the mean of the differences between now and five years ago for all city centre shops. To test the null hypothesis against the alternative, which is that the population mean difference is not 0, we need to calculate the test statistic. This is the sample mean difference, -6388.31, divided by the estimated standard error of the sample mean differences. This is the sample standard deviation of the differences, 7293.46 divided by the square root of the sample size, 10. The result is -2.77 to two places of decimals.

TABLE 2.4   Monthly footfall for 10 shops now and five years ago

Footfall now	Footfall 5 years ago	Difference
81205	83319	−2113.3
88894	85932	2961.9
89928	91439	−1511.3
96398	103161	−6763.1
101844	105055	−3211.0
103343	108996	−5652.6
103951	109183	−5232.0
105481	111493	−6011.8
105563	118298	−12734.5
107689	131303	−23614.3

We have to find the p value for this test statistic using the t distribution as the sample size is small (10). In doing this we assume that the distribution of differences is normal, or at least approximately normal. The EXCEL formula, =T.DIST(−2.77,9,TRUE) produces 0.01088. This is the probability that the test statistic is −2.77 or less. Since this is a two-sided test we need to double this probability, 0.022, to two places of decimals. This suggests only about one in 50 samples of this size will have a sample mean difference of either less than −6388.31 or more than 6388.31 *if* the null hypothesis is true. Since this p value is less than 0.05 we can reject the null hypothesis at the 5% level of significance. The population mean difference is unlikely to be 0. The sample mean difference was negative so the population mean is likely to be less than 0. We can conclude that in general the mean monthly footfall now is less than it was five years ago.

What if the two samples are not paired? Suppose that the staff at the US diner whose performance is shown in Figure 2.8 and 2.9 went on a training programme. After this the preparation times of 45 breakfasts were recorded. The mean and standard deviation of these times were 158.22 and 10.63. Has the training improved preparation times? The sample results suggest that it has, but this is only a sample. Is the mean of this sample, 158.22 significantly lower than the mean of the original sample, 165.03? To assess this we can test the null hypothesis that the population mean preparation time has not changed against the null hypothesis that the population mean is lower after the training.

The test statistic is the difference between the sample means, −6.81 (= 158.22 − 165.03) divided by the square root of the sum of the estimated sampling distribution variance. The estimated sampling distribution variance based on the original sample is 2.93 (= $12.10^2/50$) to two decimal places. The estimated sampling distribution based on the new sample is 2.51 (= $10.63^2/45$) to two decimal places. The sum of these is 5.44 and the square root of this is 2.33. The test statistic is −2.92 (= −6.81/2.33). The p value, which I obtained using =NORMDIST(−2.92,0,1,TRUE) is 0.00175. Because this test is one-sided we do not have to double this. The p value suggests if the null hypothesis is true and the population mean has not changed, a difference like −6.81 between two samples' means should only occur in one case out of 500. This is such a low chance that we can reject the null hypothesis. It seems that the training has improved the mean preparation time.

This case involves samples of 50 and 45, ie larger than 30. This means that the sampling distributions to which the sample means belong will be normal in shape. This is true whatever the shape of the population distributions. The only condition is, as in all statistical inference, that the samples should be random. If the sample sizes were less than 30 we can only test the hypothesis if both samples come from normal populations. When samples are as small as this we have to use the t distribution to benchmark our test statistic.

If we have good reason to believe that the populations from which the two samples come have the same variance we can modify the test by using a pooled or shared variance. This, being based on the combined samples, generates slightly more powerful results. The downside is that if the assumption of equal variance is wrong the results will be misleading.

Paired t and two sample hypothesis testing work if we have two samples, but what if there are more than two samples? For this we use a different approach – analysis of variance, which is usually referred to as ANOVA (ANalysis Of VAriance). The null hypothesis is that the samples come from the same population, specifically that the means of the populations they come from are the same (H_0: $\mu_1 = \mu_2 = \mu_3$ etc). The alternative hypothesis is that at least two of the samples come from populations with different means.

The test is based on the variance in the data. Variance is the sum of the squared differences between means and observations and in ANOVA is called the 'sum of squares'. The test statistic is the ratio of the mean sum of squares between the samples and the mean sum of squares within the samples. This ratio is known as F because we benchmark it against the F distribution. This is a simpler distribution to use than the z or t distributions because F, being based on squares, cannot have negative values.

Calculation of the test statistic is laborious. It involves working out both the sum of the squared differences between sample observations and their respective sample means and the weighted sum of squared differences between the sample means and the overall mean for the entire set of sample data. It is something best undertaken using statistical software. To illustrate this suppose at the US diner there are three shifts of workers. To investigate the consistency of performance the preparation times of a small sample of breakfasts served by each shift was timed. The results are shown in Figure 2.12.

FIGURE 2.12   Comparative boxplot of preparation times of breakfasts by shift

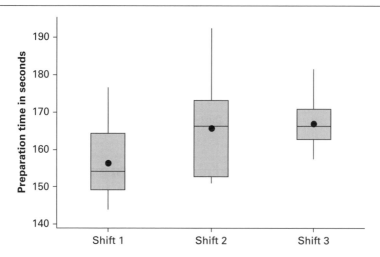

The three boxplots in Figure 2.12 differ but are the differences so significant that they suggest the population mean preparation times for the three shifts are not the same? To explore this I used the Stat/ANOVA/One-way (Unstacked) command sequence in Minitab. The results are shown in Minitab 2.1.

MINITAB 2.1   Minitab analysis of the preparation times data shown in Figure 2.12

```
One-way ANOVA: Shift 1, Shift 2, Shift 3

Source  DF    SS    MS     F      P
Factor   2   742   371   3.61  0.040
Error   28  2879   103
Total   30  3620

S = 10.14   R-Sq = 20.48%   R-Sq(adj) = 14.80%


                                Individual 95% CIs For Mean Based on
                                Pooled StDev
Level      N    Mean   StDev   ---------+---------+---------+---------+
Shift 1   12  156.36    9.71   (---------*---------)
Shift 2   10  165.76   12.65                (----------*----------)
Shift 3    9  167.01    7.08                 (---------*-----------)
                                ---------+---------+---------+---------+
                                     156.0     162.0     168.0     174.0
```

The key figure in Minitab 2.1 is the p value, 0.040 in the upper part of the output. This suggests that if the samples are from populations with the same mean there is only a 1 in 25 chance of getting sample means that differ as much as these do. Since this is less than 0.05 we can reject the null hypothesis at the 5% level of significance. We can conclude that mean performance as a whole does differ between the shifts.

The lower section of the Minitab output enables us to be more specific about our conclusion. The three bracketed broken horizontal lines are 95% confidence intervals for the population mean that each sample comes from. The top one, for shift 1, is to the left of the other two. This indicates that the population mean for shift 1 is likely to be lower than the population means for the other two shifts.

Representing non-metric data: pie charts and bar charts

The essentials of pie charts and bar charts

Pie charts are widely used to portray non-metric data. The idea is simple: to represent the frequencies of different categories within a whole as slices of a circular pie. An example is shown in Figure 2.13. In this case the whole, a sample of 110 city centre shops, is divided into categories of shop: cafés (22), clothing (14), newsagents (25), pharmacies (12), retail groceries (19) and other (37).

FIGURE 2.13   Pie chart of city centre shops by type

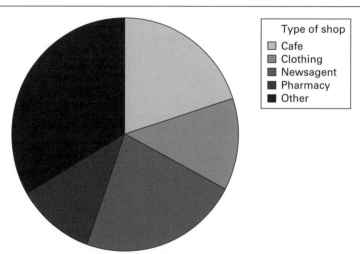

An alternative way of presenting non-metric data is the bar chart. The frequency of each category is represented by the height of its bar. Figure 2.14 shows the same data as Figure 2.13 in the form of a bar chart.

FIGURE 2.14 Bar chart of city centre shops by type

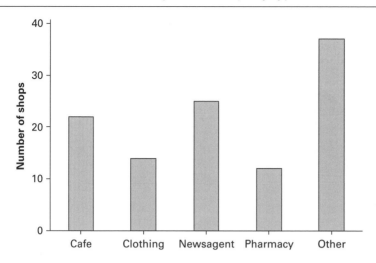

Both pie charts and bar charts are commonplace. Bar charts are more flexible tools because they can be adapted to show subdivisions within categories, as we shall see in the next chapter.

Tell me more about pie charts and bar charts

Software like Minitab enables you to control the sequence of slices. Figure 2.15 shows the same data as Figure 2.13 with the slices in order of magnitude.

FIGURE 2.15 Pie chart of city centre shops by type in order of category size

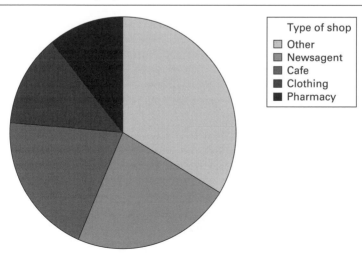

Another variation is the 'exploded' slice, which draws attention to one or more categories. Figure 2.16 has the clothing slice exploded.

FIGURE 2.16   Pie chart of city centre shops by type with exploded slice

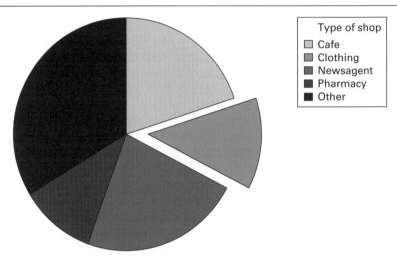

Pie charts work best when there are relatively few categories. With too many categories the diagram can begin to look like a bicycle wheel and become difficult to interpret. Figure 2.17 portrays the same data as the pie charts above but with the nine categories previously grouped together as 'Other' shown separately. As a general guide pie charts showing more than 10 categories will probably confuse the audience who you want to understand your data.

FIGURE 2.17   Pie chart of city centre shops by type with 'Other' disaggregated

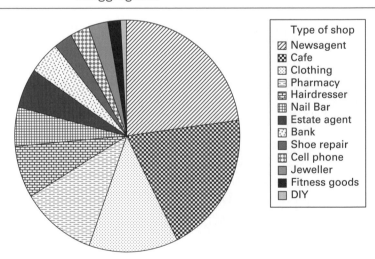

Bar charts can more easily accommodate larger numbers of categories – Figure 2.18 shows the same set of categories as Figure 2.17. Bar charts also have their limits; if you find it difficult to associate the category label with the bar that represents the category then you are probably showing too much detail.

FIGURE 2.18   Bar chart of city centre shops by type with 'Other' disaggregated

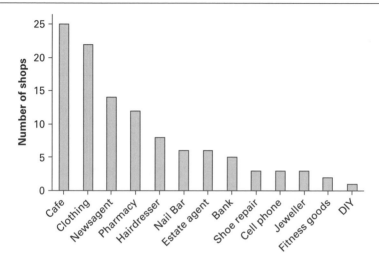

In using any diagram, including pie and bar charts, to represent data remember that it is there to do a job, to communicate your data. If you pack too much in it won't do that job for you.

Estimating and hypothesis testing of population proportions using sample proportions

The essentials of estimating and hypothesis testing of population proportions

To estimate a population proportion, represented by the Greek letter p, π (pi) you will need the sample proportion, represented by p. This is the proportion of a random sample taken from the population in the category that is of interest to us. The estimate takes the form of a confidence interval (CI) built around p. The amount added to and subtracted from p is the error.

The error has two components. The first is a value from the appropriate benchmark distribution for the sampling distribution of the sample proportions of all samples of the size of the one we have. For large samples of 100 or more this is from the z distribution. For smaller samples it should be from the binomial distribution.

The value we use depends on the level of confidence we need. The second component of the error is the sampling error. This is the standard deviation of the sampling distribution, and we estimate that using the sample proportion.

Suppose we are interested in the proportion of female employees of clothing shops. Of a random sample of 126 employees, 81 are female. The sample proportion, p is 0.643 (= 81/126) to three places of decimals. The estimated standard error is the square root of p multiplied by 1 minus p divided by the sample size, n. In mathematical terms this is $\sqrt{(p * (1 - p)/n)}$. In our example the estimated standard error is 0.043 (= $\sqrt{(0.643*0.357)/126}$) to three decimal places. For a 95% CI we multiply this by 1.96, the z value that cuts off a tail area of 2.5%. We then add and subtract the result. The resulting interval, to three decimal places is:

$$0.559 (= 0.643 - 1.96 * 0.043) \text{ to } 0.727 (= 0.643 + 1.96 * 0.043)$$

Using the binomial distribution for estimating population proportions is cumbersome as binomial distributions are specific for values of n and p. It is best left to statistical software like Minitab, where the default distribution for estimating population proportions is the binomial.

To test a hypothesis about a population proportion, state the null and alternative hypotheses, work out the test statistic and find the p value. Let's be careful here: p in 'p value' is the probability that the sample proportion occurs if the null hypothesis is true, not p for the sample proportion.

Continuing the clothing store employees case, suppose that we are told that three-quarters of all clothing shop employees are female. Does our sample data support that claim? The null hypothesis is H_0: $\pi = 0.75$ and the alternative H_1: $\pi \neq 0.75$. The test statistic is p, 0.634 minus the hypothesized value of π, 0.75 divided by the standard error. We calculate the standard error on the assumption that the null hypothesis is true, that π is 0.75. The formula is $\sqrt{(\pi * (1 - \pi)/n)}$. In our example this is 0.039 (= $\sqrt{(0.75 * 0.25)/126}$) to three places of decimals. The test statistic is –2.74 (= (0.643 – 0.75)/0.039) to two places of decimals. Using NORMDIST in EXCEL the probability of a test statistic this low or lower is 0.003 to three places of decimals. This is a two-sided test so for the p value we double this. The result, 0.006 is below 0.01 so we can reject the null hypothesis at the 1% level of significance. The sample evidence suggests that rather less than 75% of clothing shop employees are females.

Tell me more about estimating and hypothesis testing of population proportions

The amount we add to and subtract from a sample proportion to get a confidence interval (CI) for the population proportion includes a z value. The one we use depends on the level of confidence we want to have, in other words how many times out of a hundred our CI will actually include within it the population proportion. For a 95% CI our z value is 1.96. If we want to be more confident, 99%, we use 2.58. The effect of this is to widen the CI and so lose precision.

In the clothing shop employees case, the 99% CI is 0.532 (= 0.643 – 2.58 * 0.043) to 0.754 (= 0.643 + 2.58 * 0.043), or 53.2 to 75.4%, a difference of 22.2%. This is wider than the 95% CI, 0.559 to 0.727, or 55.9 to 75.4%, a difference of 19.5%. Narrower intervals are more useful than wider ones, because they provide greater precision. They give us a better idea of the likely value of the population proportion.

If increasing the level of confidence widens the CI, reducing the level of confidence narrows it. The 90% CI for the population proportion includes the z value 1.645. The CI is 0.572 (= 0.643 − 1.645 * 0.043) to 0.714 (= 0.643 + 1.645 * 0.043), or 57.2 to 71.4%, a difference of 14.2%. This is certainly more precise, but will be inaccurate once in every 10 samples.

You can pre-set precision and confidence then work out how large a sample you need. Suppose we want to estimate the population proportion of female employees in clothing shops with a 95% CI just 8% wide. The formula for the error is $z * \sqrt{(p * (1 - p)/n)}$. We don't know at the outset of our investigation what p, the sample proportion, is. We haven't decided how big our sample needs to be, let alone what the results from it are. To be on the safe side, we'll use the 'worst case' value for p, 0.5. Why is this the worst case? It produces the highest possible value for $p * (1 - p)$, 0.25. Any other value of p gives a lower result, eg if p is 0.4 $p * (1 - p)$ is 0.24, if p is 0.3 $p * (1 - p)$ is 0.21 and so on. Using any other value of p than 0.5 might result in an artificially low error. Use 0.5 and this is impossible.

The error formula is $z * \sqrt{(p * (1 - p)/n)}$. If p is 0.5 this becomes $z * \sqrt{((0.5 * 0.5)/n)}$, which simplifies to $z * \sqrt{(0.25/n)}$. Rearranging this:

from	error = $z * \sqrt{(0.25/n)}$ error/z = $\sqrt{(0.25/n)}$
to	error/(z * $\sqrt{0.25}$) = $\sqrt{(1/n)}$
to	(z * 0.5)/error = $\sqrt{n}$
to	$(z/(2 * error))^2 = n$

The z value for a 95% CI is 1.96. For an 8% CI, or 0.08 wide, the error is half that, 0.04. Dividing 1.96 by twice the error, 0.08 (= 2 * 0.04) gives 24.5. The required sample size is the square of 24.5, which is 600.25. This is a much larger figure than the size of the sample we used for our 95% CI, 126. Next time you see the results of an opinion poll look for the sample size. You'll probably find that to get accuracy to within 2 or 3% the pollsters have had to use a sample size of over 1,000.

Sometimes it is useful to test whether two samples come from populations with the same population proportion, π. The test statistic is more elaborate but the process is essentially the same as for testing that the population proportion has a particular value. To illustrate this suppose that of a random sample of 110 café employees 61 are females. Based on this and the sample of clothing shop employees, is the population proportion of females the same among café workers as it is among clothing shop workers?

The null hypothesis is that the population proportions are the same, H_0: π_{cafe} = $\pi_{clothing}$. The alternative is that they are not, H_1: $\pi_{cafe} \neq \pi_{clothing}$. The test statistic is the difference between the two sample proportions, 0.555 (= 61/110) for the café employees and 0.643 for the clothing shop employees, divided by the standard error. Since we do not have a hypothesized value for π we use the sample proportions to work out the estimated standard error. This is the elaborate bit.

We start by calculating the pooled sample proportion, which is the sum of the products of the sample proportions and the sample sizes divided by the sum of the sample sizes, 0.602 (= (0.555 * 110 + 0.643 * 126)/(110 + 126)). The estimated standard error is the square root of this divided by the sum of the reciprocals of the sample sizes, 0.064 (=$\sqrt{(0.602/(1/110 + 1/126))}$) to three decimal places. Finally, we get to the test statistic, the difference between the sample proportions, −0.088 (= 0.555 − 0.643), divided by the estimated standard error. The result is −1.38 (= −0.088/0.064) to two decimal places. The probability of a difference of −1.38 or less is 0.084 to three places of decimals. The p value is twice this, 0.168, because this is a two-sided test. Since this is not below 0.05 we can't reject H_0 and conclude that the two populations could have the same proportion. In other words the proportion of café employees that are female could be the same as the proportion of clothing shop workers that are female.

If this all sounds too complicated, it is. Let the software do the hard work: Minitab 2.2 shows the output for the test.

MINITAB 2.2   Minitab output: test and CI for two proportions

Test and CI for Two Proportions

```
Sample   X    N  Sample p
1       61  110  0.554545
2       81  126  0.642857


Difference = p (1) - p (2)
Estimate for difference:  -0.0883117
95% CI for difference:  (-0.213317, 0.0366940)
Test for difference = 0 (vs not = 0):  Z = -1.38  P-Value = 0.167
```

Analysing bivariate data

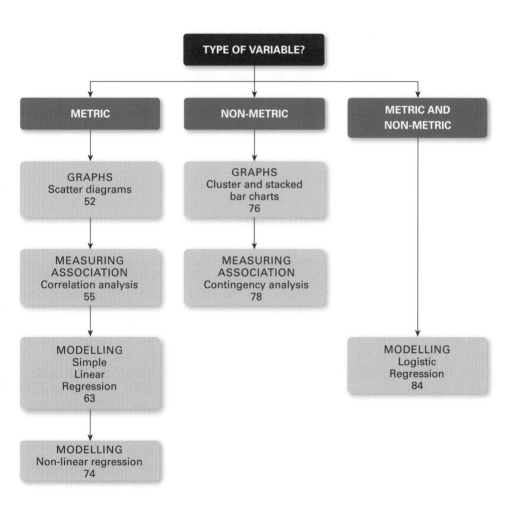

03

Topics in this chapter:

- Using scatter diagrams to portray bivariate data.

- Measuring association between variables using correlation analysis.

- Modelling relationships between metric variables using simple linear regression.

- Modelling relationships between metric variables using non-linear regression.

- Using cluster and stacked bar charts to portray two non-metric variables.

- Measuring association between non-metric variables using contingency analysis.

- Modelling relationships between metric and non-metric variables using logistic regression.

Scatter diagrams

The essentials of scatter diagrams

The reason for analysing bivariate data is to assess whether there is a connection or association between the two variables. Usually there is some reason to assume that one variable depends on the other. To reflect this, one variable is called the dependent variable and represented by the letter Y. The other variable is the independent variable and represented by X.

The best way to begin bivariate analysis is to display the data in a form that will show any evidence of a connection between the variables. This is what scatter diagrams do for two metric variables. Each variable is plotted against a numerical scale. The scale along the vertical axis is for the dependent variable, so the vertical axis is also called the Y axis. The horizontal axis is called the X axis as it has the scale for the independent variable plotted along it. Each observation, which in bivariate data consists of a pair of values, is represented by a single point. The position of the point against the vertical axis is the y value, the position against the horizontal axis the x value.

Figure 3.1 is a scatter diagram showing the numbers of visitors per month, also called the monthly footfall, at 10 shops and the floor area of the shops in square feet. The monthly footfall is plotted along the Y axis and the store area along the X axis. I have arranged them this way round as I am interested in how the footfall might depend on the store area. To put it another way, do larger shops attract more visitors? Each point in Figure 3.1 represents one shop. The point furthest to the right represents a shop that has an area of about 13,000 square feet and a monthly footfall of around 120,000.

FIGURE 3.1   Scatter diagram of the monthly footfall and store area at 10 shops

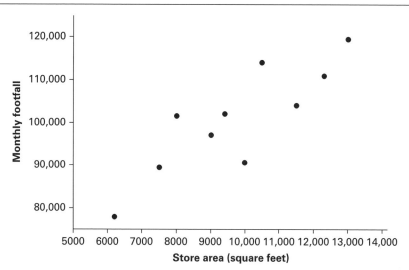

A diagram like Figure 3.1 can provide visual evidence of association but doesn't quantify the extent of association. This is the job of correlation analysis.

Tell me more about scatter diagrams

Figure 3.1 shows evidence of a direct relationship between footfall and floor area. A direct relationship is one in which lower values of one variable are associated with lower values of the other, and higher values of one variable are associated with higher values of the other. It appears from Figure 3.1 that the greater the floor area the greater the footfall.

An inverse relationship is one in which lower values of one variable are associated with higher values of the other and vice versa. Figure 3.2 shows an example of such a relationship. The preparation times for 12 'three-minute breakfasts' at a US diner are plotted on the Y axis and the years of experience of the chefs who cooked them are plotted along the X axis. The pattern in the diagram suggests that the greater the experience of the chef the less the preparation time.

Both Figure 3.1 and 3.2 suggest that the form of the relationships between the variables is linear. Although the points are not spread out along a straight line the pattern suggests a straight line would be the best way to represent the general relationship.

Figure 3.3 portrays a non-linear relationship. In this case the pattern of the scatter suggests that a straight line is not the best way to represent the relationship. The mean customer expenditure is the dependent variable and plotted on the Y axis. The store area is the independent variable and plotted on the X axis. In this case the pattern of the scatter suggests that a straight line is not the best way to represent the

FIGURE 3.2   Scatter diagram of breakfast preparation time and chef experience

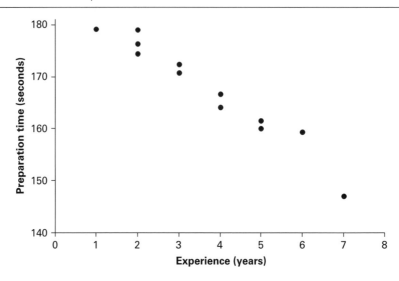

FIGURE 3.3   Scatter diagram of the mean customer expenditure and store area at 10 shops

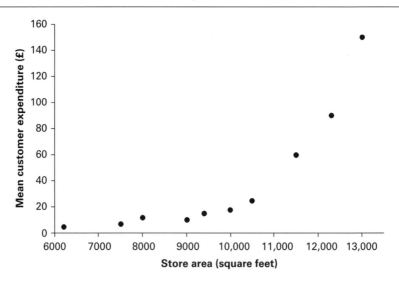

relationship. The smaller shops probably sell low value items such as newspapers, magazines or greeting cards whereas the larger shops might sell high value items like electrical goods or furniture.

Correlation analysis

The essentials of correlation analysis

Scatter diagrams show association but they don't measure it. For this we need correlation analysis. The focus of correlation analysis is the correlation coefficient, which is represented by the letter r for a sample and the Greek equivalent, ρ (rho) for a population. This measures both the strength and the direction of the association between two metric variables. It does this by comparing what is called the 'covariance' with the total scatter in the data. The covariance is a measure of the extent to which the variables co-vary, in other words how much they are 'in step' with each other. The total scatter is the amount of spread in the horizontal and vertical planes. This is measured by the product of the standard deviation of the values of the independent variable multiplied by the standard deviation of the dependent variable values.

The correlation coefficient is the covariance divided by the total scatter. Since the covariance cannot be more than the total scatter the correlation coefficient cannot be more than 1. When it is 1 the covariance matches equates to the total scatter and we have what is called 'perfect correlation', although we could also call it 'complete correlation'. The correlation coefficient is zero when the covariance is zero. The variables simply do not co-vary and we therefore have no correlation.

In practice the correlation coefficient is never exactly 1 or 0; it is always somewhere between the two. The closer it is to 1, the stronger is the relationship between the two variables. The correlation coefficient for the data in Figure 3.1 is 0.851 to three decimal places. This is fairly close to 1 so suggests good correlation in this data. The correlation coefficient for the data in Figure 3.2 to three decimal places is −0.976. This is negative, which may seem odd. In fact it is negative because the covariance is negative. The two variables, preparation time and experience, do co-vary but inversely. The maximum possible negative value of the correlation coefficient is −1. Since −0.976 is very close to this the correlation between the two variables is very strong.

The correlation coefficient for the data in Figure 3.3 is 0.845 to three decimal places. This indicates good correlation yet the strong curved pattern in the scatter suggests a stronger relationship. In this case the correlation coefficient underestimates the correlation. This is because the correlation coefficient measures linear correlation and the relationship suggested by Figure 3.3 is non-linear. It is good practice to use the correlation coefficient with a scatter diagram to make it easier to assess the type of association as well as its strength.

We can use a sample correlation coefficient, r, to test hypotheses about ρ, the population correlation coefficient. This measures the association in the population that the sample data comes from. The null hypothesis, H_0 is that there is no correlation between the X population and the Y population. The test statistic is the sample correlation coefficient times the square root of n minus 2 divided by the square root of 1 minus the square of r. Once we have this we can benchmark it against the t distribution and decide on the basis of the p value whether or not to reject the null hypothesis. This works as long as the sample is random and both the X and Y variables have normal distributions. In practice this last point means it is OK unless we have good reason to believe that X and/or Y do not have normal distributions.

Let's try this out. The sample correlation coefficient for the data shown in Figure 3.1 was 0.851. Is this significant enough for us to believe there is association between footfall and store area for all shops, ie the entire population? The test statistic is 0.851 times the square root of 8 (= 10 − 2) divided by the square root of 1 minus the square of 0.851 (= 0.724 to three decimal places). 0.851 times 2.828 (= the square root of 8 to three decimal places) is 2.407 to three decimal places, which we have to divide by the square root of 0.276 (= 1 − 0.724), which is 0.525 to three decimal places. The test statistic is 2.407 divided by 0.525, which is just over 4.58. Using =T.DIST(4.58,2,TRUE) in EXCEL gives 0.99909. This is the probability that the test statistic is lower than 4.58 and hence the probability that the correlation is less than 0.851 if there is no association in the population. Taking this away from 1 gives us 0.001. This is the p value, the probability that r is 0.851 or more if there is no association in the population. This is considerably less than the usual threshold of 0.05 for rejecting a null hypothesis so we can reject H_0. The sample correlation coefficient is highly significant and we can conclude that there is association between footfall and store area in the population. There is only a 0.001 or one in a thousand chance that a random sample that has a correlation coefficient of 0.851 or more occurs if there is 0 population correlation. This is highly unlikely so it is more logical to believe that the population correlation coefficient, ρ is not 0, and in this particular case is positive.

The square of the correlation coefficient is a widely used method of communicating the strength of the connection between metric variables. It is called the coefficient of determination and represented by R^2. The name reflects its role as a way of assessing the extent to which one variable determines another. It is usually given as a percentage and interpreted as the percentage of the variation in the dependent variable that can be explained by the variation in the independent variable. The correlation coefficient, r for the data shown in Figure 3.1 was 0.851. The square of this is 0.724 to three decimal places. An alternative way of expressing this is 72.4%; per cent means 'out of 100' so a percentage is just another way of expressing a proportion. An R^2 value of 72.4% means that 72.4% of the variation in monthly footfall can be explained by store area. This suggests there are other factors such as where the shop is and how many staff work there that might explain the other 27.6% of the footfall.

When you use either r or R^2 remember that these measures tell you that there is an association but they do not tell you why that association exists. For this you need to consider the context of the data. It could be that a modest degree of association could be spurious and no real relationship exists between the variables. A good association might arise if there is a third variable that influences your two variables.

Although both r and R^2 measure association and one is derived from the other they offer different ways of communicating association. The correlation coefficient r is particularly useful if you want to contrast positive and negative correlation. Because squares can only have positive values the coefficient of determination, R^2 cannot do this. The value of R^2 for the data in Figure 3.2 is 0.953 to three decimal places, or 95.3%. This alone does not tell you if the correlation is positive or negative.

The way in which r is calculated means that it is standardized. Dividing the covariance by the products of the standard deviations cancels out the units of measurement. The correlation coefficient for the data shown in Figure 3.2 comes from dividing a covariance calculated from values expressed in seconds (preparation time) and years (experience) by standard deviations also measured in seconds and years. Standardization of r and R^2 is very convenient because it enables us to compare association between pairs of values that are measured in different units or the same pair of values measured in different units, for instance if we used minutes for preparation time and months for experience we could get exactly the same value of r as we did with seconds and years.

Tell me more about correlation analysis

The correlation coefficient r is calculated by dividing the covariance by the standard deviation of the y values times the standard deviation of the x values. We looked at how standard deviations are calculated in the last chapter, but what about the covariance?

To get the covariance we take the deviation from the mean of the x values for each of the x values and multiply by the deviation from the mean of the y values for each of the corresponding y values. Then we add up these products and divide the result by n – 1, one less than the number of observations. We divide by n – 1 for the same reason as we do it when calculating sample standard deviations – it gives us a better estimator of the population equivalent. This is important because the reason we sample is to understand the population.

Table 3.1 shows how the covariance for the data shown in Figure 3.1 is worked out. The sum of the last column on the right, which contains the products of the deviations from the means, is 207,401,020. Divide this by the number of observations minus 1 (9) and we get 23,044,558.

To get the correlation coefficient for the data in Figure 3.1 we need the standard deviations of the areas and the footfalls. Table 3.2 contains the preparatory stages of the calculations of these.

The standard deviation of the area figures, which we'll represent as s_x to distinguish it from the other standard deviation we need, is the square root of the result of taking the sum of the squared $x - \bar{x}$ deviations, 42,164,000 and dividing by n, the number of x values minus 1, 9 (= $\sqrt{(42164000/9)}$. The result is 2,164 to the nearest whole number.

To complete this manual calculation of the correlation coefficient we need the standard deviation of the footfall figures, s_y. This is the square root of the result of taking the sum of the squared $y - \bar{y}$ deviations, 1,408,468,066 and dividing by n – 1, (= $\sqrt{(1408468066/9)}$, which is 12,510 to the nearest whole number.

The correlation coefficient for the data in Figure 3.1 is the covariance, 23044558 divided by the product of the standard deviations, 2164 and 12510, 27071640. The result, 0.851, is the same as the figure for this date in the previous section, which I obtained using Minitab.

TABLE 3.1   Calculations for the covariance of the footfall and store area data from Figure 3.1

Area (x)	Mean area ($\bar{x}$)	x − $\bar{x}$	Footfall (y)	($\bar{y}$)	y − $\bar{y}$	Mean footfall (x − $\bar{x}$)*(y − $\bar{y}$)
6,200	9740	−3540	77,967	100,752	−22,785	80,658,900
7,500	9740	−2240	89,488	100,752	−11,264	25,231,360
9,000	9740	−740	97,123	100,752	−3,629	2,685,460
8,000	9740	−1740	101,570	100,752	818	−1,423,320
9,400	9740	−340	102,029	100,752	1,277	−434,180
10,000	9740	260	90,689	100,752	−10,063	−2,616,380
11,500	9740	1760	104,063	100,752	3,311	5,827,360
10,500	9740	760	114,108	100,752	13,356	10,150,560
12,300	9740	2560	110,976	100,752	10,224	26,173,440
13,000	9740	3260	119,509	100,752	18,757	61,147,820
						207,401,020

TABLE 3.2   Calculations for the standard deviations of the footfall and store area data

Area (x)	x − $\bar{x}$	(x − $\bar{x}$)²	Footfall(y)	y − $\bar{y}$	(y − $\bar{y}$)²
6,200	−3540	12,531,600	77,967	−22,785	519,156,225
7,500	−2240	5,017,600	89,488	−11,264	126,877,696
9,000	−740	547,600	97,123	−3,629	13,169,641
8,000	−1740	3,027,600	101,570	818	669,124
9,400	−340	115,600	102,029	1,277	1,630,729
10,000	260	67,600	90,689	−10,063	101,263,969
11,500	1760	3,097,600	104,063	3,311	10,962,721
10,500	760	577,600	114,108	13,356	178,382,736
12,300	2560	6,553,600	110,976	10,224	104,530,176
13,000	3260	10,627,600	119,509	18,757	351,825,049
		42,164,000			1,408,468,066

A key skill in using correlation analysis is being able to associate values of r with patterns of scatter. A value of 1 means there is perfect positive correlation. An example of this is shown in Figure 3.4. At the other end of the scale a value of –1 means there is perfect negative correlation, as shown in Figure 3.5.

FIGURE 3.4   Scatter with a correlation coefficient (r) of 1

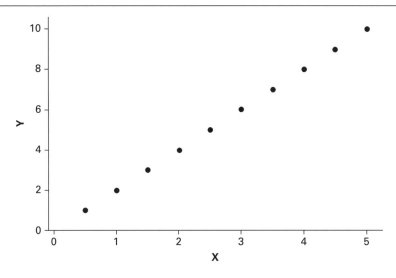

FIGURE 3.5   Scatter with a correlation coefficient (r) of –1

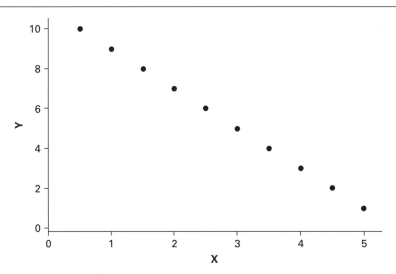

If the correlation coefficient is 0 it means there is no correlation, although to be precise no linear correlation. Figures 3.6 and 3.7 both show scatters with 0 correlation. In the case of Figure 3.6 there is no visual evidence of correlation but in Figure 3.7 there is strong evidence of non-linear correlation.

FIGURE 3.6   Scatter with a correlation coefficient (r) of 0

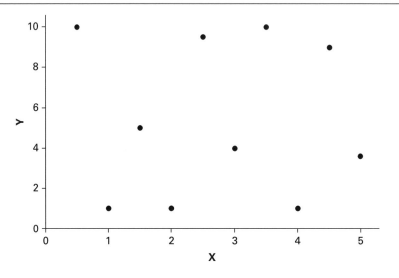

FIGURE 3.7   Scatter with a correlation coefficient (r) of 0

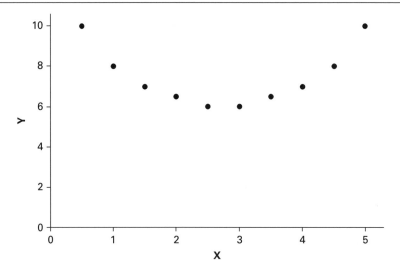

Very different scatters can produce the same correlation coefficient, which is why it is so important to look at the scatter of your data when you assess your correlation coefficient. The scatters in Figures 3.8, 3.9 and 3.10 all have the same correlation coefficient, 0.5. In the case of the data in Figure 3.8 it reflects the modest degree of association. In Figure 3.9 there is strong correlation in most of the data and the reason for the correlation coefficient being lower than we might expect is the single high outlier. In Figure 3.10 the correlation coefficient reflects the vertical clusters of y values for the x values of 0.5 and 3.

FIGURE 3.8   Scatter with a correlation coefficient (r) of 0.5

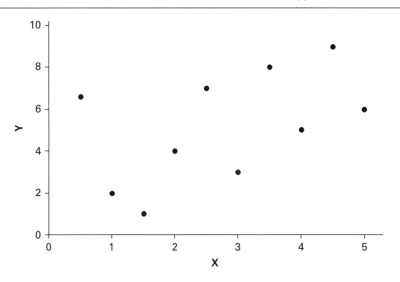

FIGURE 3.9   Scatter with a correlation coefficient (r) of 0.5 – effect of outlier

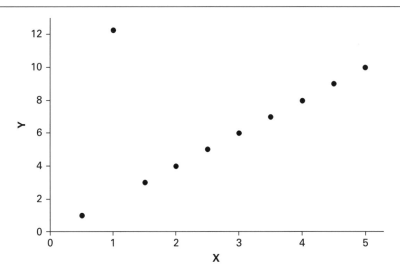

FIGURE 3.10   Scatter with a correlation coefficient (r) of 0.5 – effect of clustering

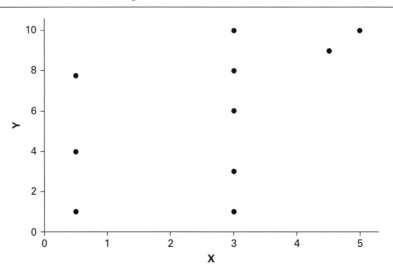

When students who use correlation in their research ask me how to interpret their results they almost always ask me how good their correlation is. I answer this in two ways. The first is very general and based on the scale of possible values of the correlation coefficient. This goes from –1 to +1. I start with whether the coefficient is positive or negative. This tells them the direction of the association, whether it is direct ie upward-sloping or inverse ie downward-sloping. I then suggest that they can describe coefficients between –1 and –0.8 or 0.8 and 1 as 'good', –0.8 to –0.5 or 0.5 to 0.8 as 'moderate', –0.5 to –0.2 or 0.2 to 0.5 as 'weak' and anything between –0.2 and 0.2 as 'negligible'. I add that they must look at the scatter. As we have seen in Figures 3.9 and 3.10 outliers and clustering will depress the value of the coefficient.

This is only a rough guide, ie downward-sloping so I advise them to test the hypothesis that the population coefficient is 0. This is better because for one thing the p value quantifies the significance of the sample coefficient and for another it brings sample size into consideration. Why is sample size important? Look at Figure 3.11.

The correlation coefficient for the data in Figure 3.11 is 0.851. This is exactly the same as the correlation coefficient for the footfalls and store area data shown in Figure 3.1. When we tested the hypothesis that the population correlation coefficient ρ for footfall and store area was 0 we rejected it. The p value was 0.002.

The formula for the test statistic, t, used to test H_0: $\rho = 0$ applied to the correlation coefficient for the data in Figure 3.11 is:

$$t = \frac{r * \sqrt{(n-2)}}{\sqrt{(1-r^2)}} = \frac{0.851 * \sqrt{(3-2)}}{\sqrt{(1-0.851^2)}} = \frac{0.851 * \sqrt{1}}{\sqrt{(1-0.724)}} = \frac{0.851}{\sqrt{0.276}} = \frac{0.851}{0.525}$$

= 1.621 to 3 decimal places

FIGURE 3.11   Scatter with a correlation coefficient (r) of 0.851

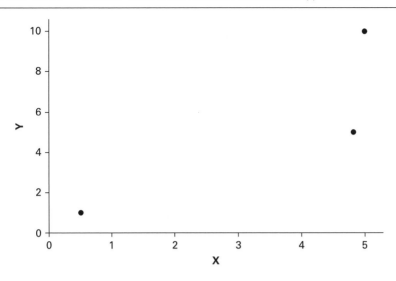

In EXCEL = T.DIST(1.621,2,TRUE) produces 0.824 to three decimal places. This is the probability of the test statistic being less than 1.621. The probability that the test statistic is 1.621 or more is 1 − 0.824, which is 0.176. This is the p value, the probability of r being 0.851 or more if there is no association in the population. It tells us that if there is no correlation in the population we can expect a correlation coefficient of 0.851 or more approximately one in every six samples (1/0.176 ≈ 1/6). Our conclusion is that we cannot reject H_0; the population correlation coefficient could well be 0. How can this be? We had the same sample correlation coefficient, 0.851 for the footfall and store area data in Figure 3.1 but then we rejected the null hypothesis of no population correlation. The answer is that we had more observations in Figure 3.1 – there were 10 observations in Figure 3.1 but only three in Figure 3.11. With only three observations the correlation coefficient is very fragile. If we had one more observation it would probably change the picture considerably, while one more observation in Figure 3.1 is unlikely to have such a dramatic effect. When it comes to statistical hypothesis testing, sample size matters.

Simple linear regression

The essentials of simple linear regression

Correlation analysis tells you whether there is association between two metric variables. Regression tells you what form that association takes. Simple linear regression is the most basic regression method. It is simple because it is used to model the connection between just two variables and linear because the models it generates take the form of straight lines.

Any straight line plotted on a pair of axes consisting of an x axis and a y axis can be described using an equation. The form of the equation is Y = a + bX. The intercept, which is the starting point of the line on the y axis, is represented by a, and the slope, the gradient at which the line travels, is represented by b. If b is positive the line slopes upwards, if it is negative the line slopes downwards.

Simple linear regression finds the straight line that best fits the scatter. Unless the scatter is perfectly correlated there are many lines that could be plotted through it. The best fit line is the one that has the least differences between the points in the scatter. The points can be above or below the line; these differences can be negative or positive. This means that if we simply added up the differences the negative and positive ones could cancel each other out. To avoid this problem simple linear regression is based on the squares of the differences. It uses calculus to find the line that traces a path through the scatter that has the lowest possible sum of squared differences between itself and the points in the scatter. This is called the 'regression line' or 'best fit line'. Because it is based on minimizing the squared differences the technique is also known as 'least squares regression'.

Using simple linear regression involves applying two equations to the data. One of these determines the slope, the other the intercept. These equations are:

For the slope:

$$b = \frac{\Sigma xy - (\Sigma x * \Sigma y)/n}{\Sigma x^2 - (\Sigma x)^2/n}$$

And for the intercept:

$$a = (\Sigma y - b * \Sigma x)/n$$

I am showing you these to emphasize that the results come directly from all the data. Σx is the sum of all the x values and Σy the sum of all the y values. The other ingredient in this mathematical recipe is n, the number of observations.

In practice we wouldn't use these equations to work out the line of best fit. We would use software in which they are embedded. To get the slope of the regression line for the footfall and store area data shown in Figure 3.1 I put the y and x values into columns A and B of an EXCEL spreadsheet. In the formula bar I typed =SLOPE(A1:A10,B1:B10). The result was 4.918 to three places of decimals.

To get the intercept I typed =INTERCEPT(A1:A10,B1:B10) in the formula bar. The result was 52842 to the nearest whole number. The equation that describes the regression line, which is called the 'regression equation', is:

Y = 52842 + 4.918X or, more specifically:
monthly footfall = 52842 + 4.918 store area

This is the regression model of the relationship between footfall and store area. It suggests that beginning at 52,842 square feet, for every extra square foot we would expect the footfall to increase by approximately five. Figure 3.12 shows the regression line plotted through the scatter.

FIGURE 3.12   The best fit line for the data from Figure 3.1

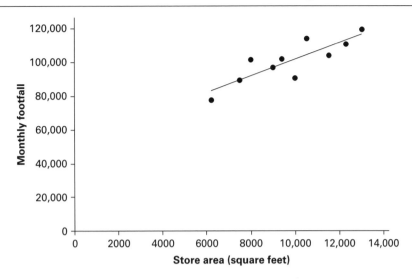

Notice that although I have started both scales in Figure 3.12 at 0 I have not extended the line to the vertical axis. This is because the line is based on the plotted data that occupies a range of store area from about 6,000 to about 13,000 square feet. Extending the line outside this range is purely speculative. For all we know the line may plummet or soar outside this range rather than continue along the same linear path. We simply do not have the data to be able to tell.

Tell me more about simple linear regression

Although EXCEL produces regression equations, statistical software offers a more comprehensive regression toolkit. I used Minitab to produce the output in Minitab 3.1 for the data shown in Figure 3.12.

The regression equation has a positive intercept, 186 but a negative slope, −5.13. I have plotted this equation in Figure 3.13. Notice that the line misses most of the points in the scatter. This is of no concern. A best fit line is the one that is as close as possible to all the points and doesn't have to go through any of them.

The table section of the output below the regression equation includes p values for the two coefficients, 'Coef' of the regression equation, the intercept, which Minitab refers to as the Constant; and the slope, which is what Minitab refers to using the independent variable name, in this case Experience. Both p values are 0 to three places of decimals. These tell us that the coefficients of the regression equation for this sample of data are significant. In other words, it is very unlikely given these sample results that the regression equation for the entire population would have an intercept of 0 or a slope of 0.

Lower down in the output is another p value under Analysis of Variance. This assesses the overall significance of the model rather than the individual coefficients.

MINITAB 3.1   Regression analysis: Preparation time versus Experience

```
The regression equation is:
Preparation time (seconds) = 186 - 5.13 Experience (years)


Predictor      Coef   SE Coef       T       P
Constant     186.397    1.479   126.05   0.000
Experience   -5.1333    0.3640   -14.10   0.000


S = 2.20438    R-Sq = 95.2%    R-Sq(adj) = 94.7%


Analysis of Variance

Source           DF        SS       MS       F       P
Regression        1    966.21   966.21  198.84   0.000
Residual Error   10     48.59     4.86
Total            11   1014.81
```

FIGURE 3.13   The best fit line for the data from Figure 3.2

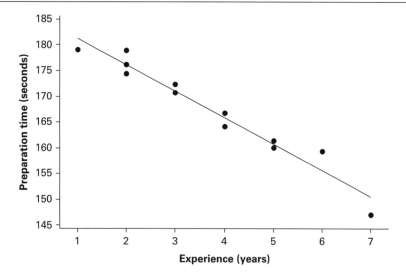

Since it is 0 to three places of decimals the model is strong enough to suggest that it is extremely unlikely that there is no such model for the population.

If you look carefully at the output you will see 'R-Sq' and 'R-Sq(adj)'. These are respectively the coefficient of determination, R^2 and an adjusted version of it, which is slightly lower. The adjustment allows for the random association that could exist between the two variables so R-Sq(adj) is a more cautious measure of the association in the data. The S to the left of the R-Sq is a measure of the spread of the points around the best fit line, the standard error of the regression. The lower this is, the better the model.

The heading above Constant and Experience is Predictor. This is because one of the main uses of regression models is to predict values of Y for given values of X. The easiest way to make a prediction is to insert the x value and use the equation to work out the corresponding y value. Suppose we need to estimate the monthly footfall for a shop with an area of 11,000 square feet. Our prediction is:

Monthly footfall = 52842 + 4.918 * 11000 = 52842 + 54098 = 106940

Similarly we can estimate the monthly footfall of a shop with an area of 10,000:

Monthly footfall = 52842 + 4.918 * 10000 = 52842 + 49180 = 102022

There is a shop in our sample that does actually have an area of 10,000 square feet and it has a monthly footfall of 90,689. This is lower than our predicted value of 102,022. The difference is known as a 'residual'. The analysis of residuals is an important adjunct to regression analysis, as I will explain later on.

Why, you might ask, are the estimated value and the observed value different? This is because the line is the general regression model based on the sample data collectively, and individual observations may stray from this model. In fact if we looked at the entire population of shops there would probably be many with an area of 10,000 square feet and it would be odd if they all had exactly the same monthly footfall.

FIGURE 3.14   Regression plot of the data from Figure 3.1 with the distribution of footfalls for shops with 10,000 square feet areas

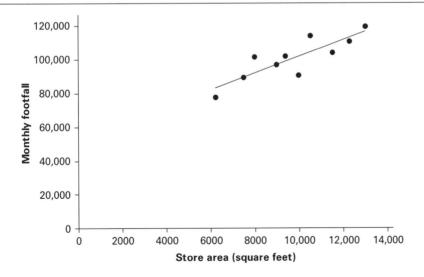

One of the assumptions on which simple linear regression is based is that the residuals for the y values associated with an x value are normally distributed with a mean of 0. To illustrate this using the footfall and area data in Figure 3.14, I have inserted a normal distribution vertically across the regression line above 10,000 on the horizontal scale. The point on the line above 10,000 is the mean of that normal distribution so our estimate is in fact an estimate of the mean monthly footfall of all shops with an area of 10,000 square feet. It is only a point estimate, a single figure. The disadvantage of point estimates is that we have no idea of how likely they are to be correct, in other words we do not know how much confidence we can have in the estimate.

It is possible to calculate a confidence interval for the population mean of the y values associated with a specific x value. The calculation involves a t value and a standard error, as we would do to estimate a population mean from the mean of a small sample. This is rather laborious so it is better to use software. I used Minitab to produce a confidence interval for the population mean monthly footfall of shops with an area of 10,000 square feet. The results are shown in Minitab 3.2.

MINITAB 3.2   Predicted values for new observations

```
New Obs      Fit      SE Fit 95% CI            95% PI
   1         102031   2221   (96910, 107152)   (85169, 118893)


Values of Predictors for New Observations

New Obs    Area
   1       10000
```

The new observation, 'New Obs' is 10,000. The 'Fit' is the point estimate. At 102,031 it differs slightly from the value I calculated from the equation. This is because I rounded the coefficients a little and Minitab used the precise ones. Under '95% CI' we have the confidence interval. This tells us that we can be 95% confident that the population mean monthly footfall for shops with an area of 10,000 square feet is somewhere between 96,910 and 107,152.

To the right of the output is another interval estimate, under '95% PI'. This is a prediction interval. It is an interval estimate of the monthly footfall of a single shop with an area of 10,000 square feet. It tells us that we can be 95% confident that the monthly footfall of a shop with this area is between 85,169 and 118,893. Notice that it is much wider than the confidence interval. This is because it is based on a distribution of individual values not a sampling distribution, and sampling distributions are more compact.

There are a number of assumptions about the residual parts of y values, which are the differences between the points and the line that should be true for simple linear regression to be valid. The residuals should be values of a random variable. If they are not, there is some other factor at work in our data and we should try and bring it into the model. They should be symmetrically distributed around the line with a mean of 0. The spread of the distributions of residuals for the range of y values should be constant. Figure 3.15 shows a scatter where this is not true. It is an example of what is called 'heteroscedasticity'. Because the spread in the y values increases from left to right it is positive heteroscedasticity. Negative heteroscedasticity is where the spread in the y values decreases from left to right. If you do have heteroscedasticity in your data it is still possible to produce a regression model but its presence suggests there is something else shaping the patterns in your data.

FIGURE 3.15   Scatter with positive heteroscedasticity

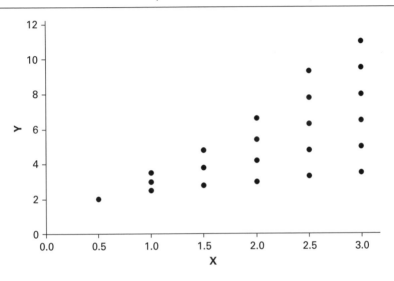

Analysing the residuals, which are the parts of the y values that the model doesn't explain, is how we can ascertain whether the assumptions hold. Figure 3.16 is a histogram of the residuals from the regression model of the monthly footfall and shop area data shown in Figure 3.12. I have superimposed a normal curve to allow us to consider whether the assumption about the normality of the residuals is met. Although the histogram is not a perfect fit to the normal curve there is a broad alignment with it. We can conclude that the normality assumption is likely to be met.

Figure 3.17 is a scatter diagram of the residuals of the model in Figure 3.12 plotted against the predicted values of the footfall. What we are looking for here is evidence of uneven spread across the range of the footfall data and patterns in the residuals that might suggest we need to consider changing the model. In fact in the scatter in Figure 3.17 there seems to be no evidence of uneven spread or pattern.

The data in Figure 3.15 does exhibit uneven scatter. Figure 3.18 shows the best fit regression line superimposed on the data. The histogram of the residuals of this model is shown in Figure 3.19. They form a normal distribution so the assumption of normality appears to be met. The scatter diagram of the residuals and fitted y

FIGURE 3.16   Histogram of the residuals from the regression model in Figure 3.12

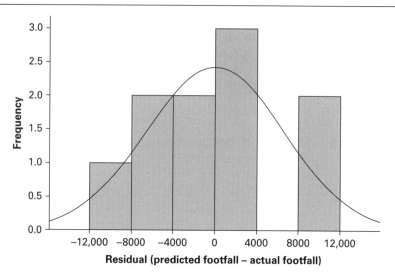

Residual (predicted footfall – actual footfall)

FIGURE 3.17   Scatter diagram of the residuals and predicted footfalls from the regression model in Figure 3.12

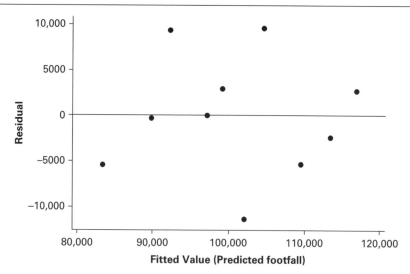

Fitted Value (Predicted footfall)

values in Figure 3.20 shows that there is an uneven spread, with increasing spread from the left to the right of the horizontal axis.

The scatter in Figure 3.3, the mean customer expenditure and shop area, is not linear. This is evident from Figure 3.21, which has the best fit linear regression model superimposed on the scatter.

FIGURE 3.18 The regression model for the data in Figure 3.15

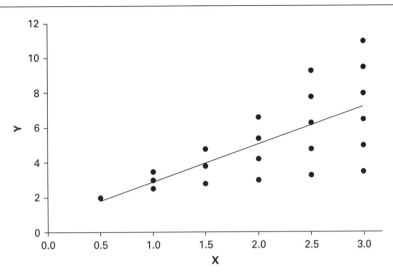

FIGURE 3.19 Histogram of the residuals from the regression model in Figure 3.18

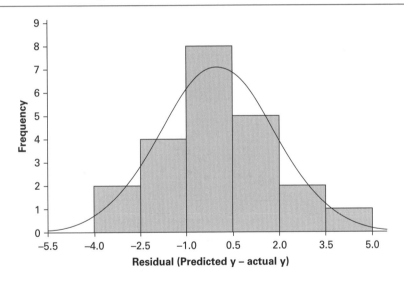

Figure 3.22 is a histogram of the residuals of the regression model in Figure 3.21 with a superimposed normal curve. The pattern is distinctly skewed and not normal, which suggests that the assumption of normality of residuals is unlikely to be met.

Figure 3.23 is a scatter diagram of the residuals and the predicted expenditure figures from the regression model in Figure 3.21. There is a clear pattern to the

FIGURE 3.20   Scatter diagram of the residuals from the regression
model in Figure 3.18

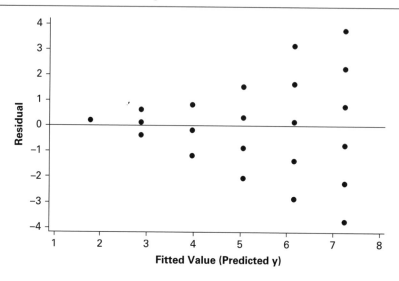

FIGURE 3.21   The regression model for the data in Figure 3.3

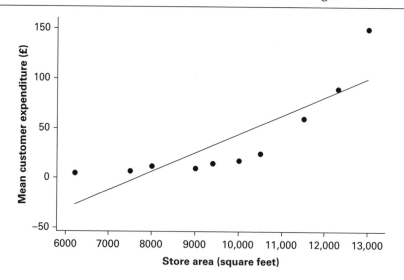

scatter with higher residuals for lower and higher predictions but lower residuals for
the predictions in the middle. This and the non-normality in Figure 3.22 demonstrate
that the simple linear regression fit in Figure 3.21 is not the most appropriate model
for the data. Rather than a straight line model, the pattern in the scatter suggests we
should look to non-linear regression for a better fit.

FIGURE 3.22 Histogram of the residuals from the regression model in Figure 3.21

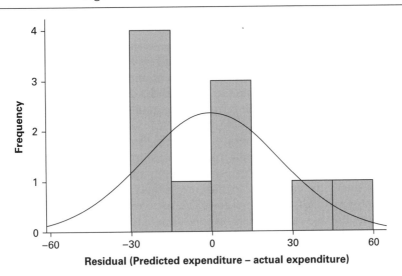

Residual (Predicted expenditure – actual expenditure)

FIGURE 3.23 Scatter diagram of the residuals and predicted expenditure from the regression model in Figure 3.21

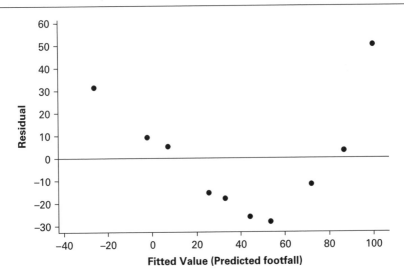

Fitted Value (Predicted footfall)

Non-linear regression

The essentials of non-linear regression

The purpose of non-linear regression is the same as that of simple linear regression: to find the best fit model for metric bivariate data. The approach, minimizing the sum of squared errors, is common to simple linear and non-linear regression.

The key difference between simple linear and non-linear regression is that in simple linear regression the search is for the one model that will best fit the data. In non-linear regression there is a choice of non-linear models and the method used to find the best-fit model involves steps or iterations. To use non-linear regression we have to decide which model to apply and provide starting values for the coefficients. It is possible to use simple linear regression to apply some non-linear models. We can do this by changing the data using logarithms. In this process, known as 'transformation' in effect we straighten the data to enable us to use simple linear regression.

To illustrate the two approaches I'll apply them to the mean customer expenditure and shop area data shown in Figure 3.3. The shape of the scatter suggests an exponential curve might be appropriate: from the left of the scatter there is at first a gradual then a substantial increase in y values. I produced the model shown in Figure 3.24 using Minitab. I selected the exponential model from the menu of non-linear regression models and entered starting values of 0 for the coefficients, the intercept and slope. The equation of the best fit exponential model was:

Mean customer expenditure (£) = 0.029 * EXP(0.00066 * Store Area)

The coefficients have small values because the values of the independent variable, Store Area, are large. Another way of expressing this equation is to express the exponent as a power of Euler's constant (2.718 to three decimal places) which is the base of natural logarithms:

Mean customer expenditure (£) = $0.029 * 2.718^{(0.00066 * \text{Store Area})}$

The model in Figure 3.24 looks a better fit than the linear model applied to the same data in Figure 3.21. This impression is backed up by the size of S, the standard error of the regression, which was 26.984 for the model in Figure 3.21 and is a much lower 3.895 for the model in Figure 3.24.

To use the transformations method we need to start with the general expression for an exponential curve, $Y = a * b^X$. This is not linear as it involves a power; X, the independent variable is the exponent of the slope, b. Logarithms use powers to perform complicated arithmetic in simpler ways by changing the ways the numbers are represented. In short they made it possible to multiply without multiplying. In the past this was invaluable, but now computer software and calculators have made this less important although they are still useful in non-linear regression.

Simple linear regression finds best fit models of the general form $Y = a + bX$ not $Y = a * b^X$. It can only help us find a best fit exponential model if we can make $Y = a * b^X$ like $Y = a + bX$. This is what logarithms can do; $Y = a * b^X$ becomes

FIGURE 3.24 The non-linear regression model for the data in Figure 3.3

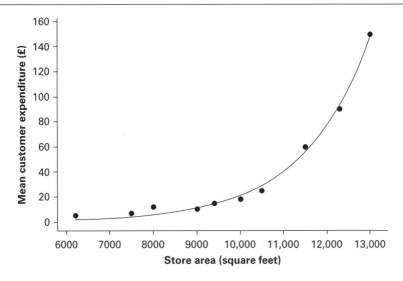

log Y = log a + X log b. Rather than using simple linear regression to analyse Y against X we need to use it to analyse log Y against X. If we transform the y values into log y values, which statistical software such as Minitab can do, we can use simple linear regression to find an exponential model to fit the data. Figure 3.25 shows the area values from Figure 3.3 and the associated expenditure values transformed with the superimposed line of best fit.

FIGURE 3.25 Scatter diagram of the transformed data from Figure 3.3 with line of best fit

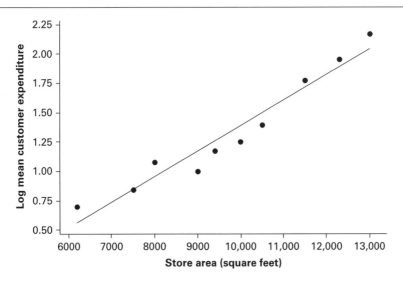

The equation of the line in Figure 3.25 is:

Log Mean customer expenditure (£) = –1.83 + 0.0005 Store area

By anti-logging –1.83 and 0.0005 we can express the relationship in terms of Y rather than log Y. The anti-logs are 0.16 and 1.0005, so it is:

Mean customer expenditure (£) = –1.83 * $1.0005^{\text{Store area}}$

The R^2 value for this model is 94.2%, which is considerably better than the 71.3% for the model in Figure 3.21. Note that we cannot use S, the standard error of the regression, to compare these two models as the form of the dependent variable is not the same; it is £ in the first case and logs in the second.

Tell me more about non-linear regression

It is not possible to use transformation for all types of non-linear relationships. In some cases, like the exponential model, there is a choice between non-linear modelling and linear modelling of transformed data. In these cases, which is better? You probably need more mathematical knowledge to use non-linear modelling but the repertoire of models available in software such as Minitab is wider. Transformation is for many people more accessible because it uses simple linear regression. It also enables you to compare models using R^2, which is not the case with non-linear regression.

The least squares method we have used to obtain simple linear regression models can be used for data that can be transformed to a linear pattern using logarithms. Non-linear regression like the method we used to find the model shown in Figure 3.24 uses different approaches, which is why we did not get the same equation for the best fit line shown in Figure 3.24 as for the one shown in Figure 3.25.

There is a variety of non-linear models. Minitab offers a menu of two dozen or so. In my experience these types of models are rarely relevant to data that typically arises in business projects. I last used it in modelling output and energy consumption in paper-making some time ago. There are applications in economics such as in average cost curves but in practice the range of the data is generally so limited that non-linear effects tend to be imperceptible. If you want to look into non-linear bivariate regression in more detail I recommend Bates and Watts (2007) or Seber and Wild (2003).

Cluster and stacked bar charts

The essentials of cluster and stacked bar charts

If you want to look at association between two non-metric variables the best way to start is by arranging your data in a two-way table. Because the purpose of such a table is to enable us to look at whether one variable is dependent, or contingent upon another this type of table is also known as a 'contingency table'.

Table 3.3 summarizes the results from a Likert scale question in a questionnaire about consumer satisfaction with the quality of food served in a restaurant and the gender of the respondents.

TABLE 3.3   Responses to 'Food quality in this restaurant is good' by gender of respondent

Gender	Strongly agree	Agree	Neither agree nor disagree	Disagree	Strongly disagree	Total
Female	2	16	11	16	5	50
Male	7	25	7	10	1	50
Total	9	41	18	26	6	100

FIGURE 3.26   Cluster bar chart of the data in Table 3.3

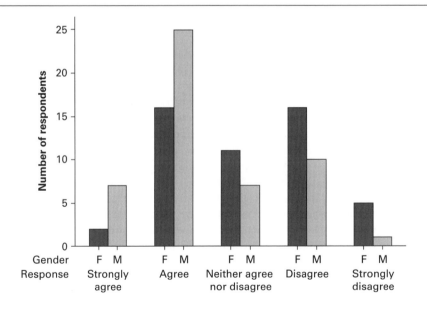

There are two types of bar chart that we could use to show this data. Figure 3.26 is a cluster bar chart and Figure 3.27 is a stacked bar chart. Both figures indicate there is an imbalance of responses between the two genders. In Figure 3.26 the pairs of bars are not of the same height. More males than females agree or strongly agree and more females than males disagree or strongly disagree. In Figure 3.27 the stacks for each response category are not evenly divided by gender.

FIGURE 3.27 Stacked bar chart of the data in Table 3.3

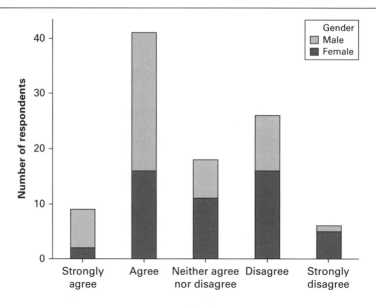

Tell me more about cluster and stacked bar charts

Figures 3.26 and 3.27 do essentially the same job: they allow us to ascertain how the responses vary by gender. One will usually suffice, but which one should you choose? It depends on the emphasis you want to put on the data. If I want to highlight the distribution of female responses compared to the distribution of male responses, the cluster bar chart in Figure 3.26 would be better. This would help me to communicate the inclination of males to be positive about the food quality as the bars that represent the responses from males is skewed with the majority to the left of the chart. In contrast the bars representing the responses from females are more symmetrical across the categories of response.

The stacked bar chart in Figure 3.27 would be more useful if I want to convey the contrasting divisions within each response category. The stacked bars representing the positive responses have larger upper components, representing responses from males, than lower components, representing the female. The stacked bars representing the negative responses have in contrast larger lower components, indicating that the females are more critical about the food quality.

Contingency analysis

The essentials of contingency analysis

Contingency analysis allows us to test the strength of the association between two non-metric variables; specifically it tests the null hypothesis of no association against the alternative of some association. A key assumption is that the data we use to conduct a contingency test is from a random sample of a population. The hypotheses allow us to assess whether any association in our sample data is strong enough to suggest that there is association in the population.

The test statistic is based on the difference between the actual numbers in each box or cell in the contingency table, the 'observed values' (O), and the numbers that we would anticipate if there were no association in the data, the 'expected values' (E). The differences have to be squared, to avoid negative and positive differences cancelling each other out and standardized before being added together. The resulting figure is the test statistic. Standardization involves dividing each squared difference by the expected value for the cell. The purpose of this is to allow us to benchmark the test statistic against the benchmark distribution for contingency testing, the chi-square (χ^2) distribution. This will give us the p value that we can use to assess the validity of the null hypothesis.

We can use this procedure to test the hypothesis of no association in the data in Table 3.3. The hypotheses are:

H_0: There is no association in the population between response to the food quality question and gender.

H_1: There is some association in the population between response to the food quality question and gender.

Table 3.4 shows the data from Table 3.3 (O) with expected values (E), squared differences $(O-E)^2$ and standardized values $(O-E)^2/E$ for each cell. The expected

TABLE 3.4 Observed, expected values and standardized contributions to χ^2 for the data in Table 3.3

	Strongly agree	Agree	Neither agree nor disagree	Disagree	Strongly disagree	Total
Females (O)	2	16	11	16	5	50
Females (E)	4.50	20.50	9.00	13.00	3.00	50.00
$(O-E)^2$	6.25	20.25	4.00	9.00	4.00	
$(O-E)^2/E$	1.39	0.99	0.44	0.69	1.33	
Males (O)	7	25	7	10	1	50
Males (E)	4.50	20.50	9.00	13.00	3.00	50.00
$(O-E)^2$	6.25	20.25	4.00	9.00	4.00	
$(O-E)^2/E$	1.39	0.99	0.44	0.69	1.33	

values are based on the row and column totals. The sample of 100 respondents is split evenly by gender with 50 females and 50 males. If there is no association between type of response and gender we would expect the responses for each category to also be evenly divided by gender. This means that the nine respondents who strongly agreed would be divided 50:50 ie 4.5 females and 4.5 males. It doesn't matter that these are not whole numbers and are therefore not feasible. They are the mean figures we would expect from all samples of this size with the same distribution of responses.

The standardized value for each cell, $(O–E)^2/E$ is the contribution that the cell makes to the test statistic, which is the value of χ^2 calculated from the data. If we add them all up they come to 9.68 (= 1.39 + 0.99 + 0.44 + 0.69 + 1.33 + 1.39 + 0.99 + 0.44 + 0.69 + 1.33).

The next question is whether this test statistic is significant, in other words large enough to suggest we should reject the null hypothesis of no association. We need to compare it to the χ^2 distribution. This is complicated by the fact that the χ^2 distribution comes in different versions. The one we use depends on the number of degrees of freedom in our data. This is the number of columns in our contingency minus one times the number of rows minus one. In Table 3.3 there were five columns of data and two rows of data so the number of degrees of freedom is four.

The χ^2 distribution with four degrees of freedom is shown in Figure 3.28. It is a probability distribution so the total area under the curve is one. It shows the distribution of test statistics we would get if we analysed all possible samples that we could have got if the null hypothesis were true. The value of the test statistic from the analysis in Table 3.4 is marked on the horizontal axis. The shaded area to the right of it represents the probability that we get a test statistic of 9.68 or higher. This area is 0.04618, or 4.618% of the total area. This is the p value, and since in this case it is less than 0.05, or 5% we can reject the null hypothesis at the 5% level of significance. It appears that there is some association: females and males exhibit different patterns of response to the food quality question.

FIGURE 3.28   The χ^2 distribution with four degrees of freedom

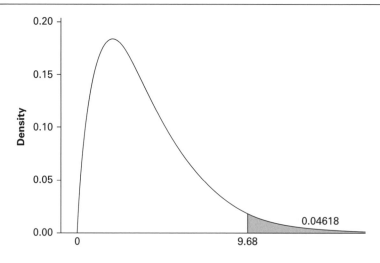

A potential difficulty in contingency testing occurs if any of the expected values are small. For the test to work, all the expected values in the contingency table should be more than 1, and preferably more than 5. Some of the expected values in Table 3.4 are less than 5, which means that we need to exercise some caution in interpreting the result. The problem can be solved by either combining cells or collecting more data.

Tell me more about contingency analysis

The number of degrees of freedom that we use to pick the correct version of the Chi-square distribution reflects the size of the contingency table; the more rows and columns in the table the greater the number of degrees of freedom. But why the number of rows less 1 times the number of columns minus 1? Let me illustrate this with Table 3.5, which has just four of the 10 values and the row and column totals from Table 3.3; the rest of the table is blank.

TABLE 3.5   Selected values and row and column total from Table 3.3

Gender	Strongly agree	Agree	Neither agree nor disagree	Disagree	Strongly disagree	Total
Female	2	16				50
Male				10	1	50
Total	9	41	18	26	6	

If you didn't know the rest of the values it wouldn't matter. With just four you can fill in the blanks. This is because once we have specified four values – and it could be any four – you have no freedom to choose what any of the other values are. Try it. The males who strongly agree have to number 7 otherwise the Strongly agree column total cannot be 9. Similarly the number of males who agree has to be 25, and so on. If I had only specified three values you would have freedom to choose the fourth, in other words to exercise the fourth degree of freedom.

The table size, the number of rows and columns, and the consequent number of degrees of freedom, is a key issue in contingency testing. The more cells in the table the more Observed/Expected differences there will be and hence the greater spread in the possible test statistic values if the null hypothesis is true. Samples are not clones; they do vary and it is very unlikely that in any one sample there will be a complete match between the Observed and Expected values. The small differences that will arise as a result of the variation inherent in sampling may give rise to a test statistic that will wrongly seem significant if we use the χ^2 distribution with too few degrees of freedom, and wrongly seem not significant if we use χ^2 distribution with too many degrees of freedom.

Because it is based on squared differences the test statistic will always be positive. The larger the differences between the Observed and Expected values the bigger the test statistic will be and vice versa. Small differences will result in low test statistics and not rejecting the null hypothesis of no association. This is logical because the Expected values assume no association and so the closer the Observed values are to their corresponding Expected values the less evidence we have for association.

If we do have a significantly large test statistic, one that leads us to reject the null hypothesis, we can conclude that there is likely to be association. This is a little vague. We can dig deeper and consider why the association arises. To do this we need to consider the components of the test statistic and ask what makes it significantly large. In Table 3.4 the largest components of the test statistic of 9.68 are the two values of 1.39 and the two values of 1.33. Together these make up over half (5.44) of the test statistic yet are only four of the ten components. They arise because of the imbalance in the extreme responses. Far more males (7) than females (2) Strongly agree and far more females (5) than males (1) Strongly disagree.

The example I have used to illustrate contingency analysis is fairly simple, with only 10 cells. Often such analysis is more elaborate. Even in my example if we had distinguished between adult females and girls, and adult males and boys we would have had 20 cells in the contingency table. The laborious nature of the arithmetic processes involved make contingency analysis something you should do using computer software. I used the tables facility on the Stat menu in Minitab to generate an analysis of the data in Table 3.5; see Minitab 3.3.

MINITAB 3.3 Chi-square Test: Strongly agree, Agree, Neither agree nor disagree, Disagree, Strongly disagree

Expected counts are printed below observed counts
Chi-Square contributions are printed below expected counts

	Strongly agree	Agree	Neither agree nor disagree	Disagree	Strongly disagree	Total
Females	2	16	11	16	5	50
	4.50	20.50	9.00	13.00	3.00	
	1.389	0.988	0.444	0.692	1.333	
Males	7	25	7	10	1	50
	4.50	20.50	9.00	13.00	3.00	
	1.389	0.988	0.444	0.692	1.333	
Total	9	41	18	26	6	100

Chi-Sq = 9.694, DF = 4, P-Value = 0.046
4 cells with expected counts less than 5.

The test statistic 'Chi-Sq' figure of 9.694 is slightly different from the 9.68 I reached by calculation. This is because in my arithmetic I rounded the figures to two decimal places whereas Minitab uses precise figures throughout.

The last line of the Minitab Chi-Square test output above is '4 cells with expected counts less than 5'. This is a warning that the data is spread too thinly in some parts of the table. The implication is that the test result is not completely reliable. It is a 'yellow card' so Minitab has still carried out the test. If any of the expected values were less than 1 it would not conduct the test as the results would definitely be unreliable.

What is worrying Minitab is the low Expected values for Strongly agree (4.50 and 4.50) and Strongly disagree (3.00 and 3.00). We can get around the problem and generate reliable results by combining categories. This has to make sense. It would be illogical, for instance, to combine Strongly agree with Strongly disagree as they are completely different responses to the food quality question. The best solution is to combine Strongly agree and Agree, and Disagree and Strongly disagree. The first of these combinations represents agreement and the second disagreement. The data consolidated in this way is in Table 3.6.

TABLE 3.6   Data from Table 3.5 with combined cells

Gender	Strongly agree/Agree	Neither agree nor disagree	Disagree/Strongly disagree	Total
Female	18	11	21	50
Male	32	7	11	50
Total	50	18	32	100

The Minitab analysis of the revised table is shown in Minitab 3.4. As the table is now smaller the number of degrees of freedom, 'DF' in the Minitab output is lower. There is now no warning message at the end of the output so the results are reliable. The p value at 0.019 is considerably lower than 0.05 so we can reject the null hypothesis of no association at the 5% level of significance. Our conclusion is that there is some association between gender and responses to the food quality question.

MINITAB 3.4 Chi-square Test: Strongly agree/Agree, Neither agree nor disagree, Disagree/Strongly disagree

```
Expected counts are printed below observed counts
Chi-Square contributions are printed below expected counts

                              Neither
               Strongly     agree nor        Disagree/
             agree/Agree     disagree  Strongly disagree    Total
Females           18            11               21           50
                25.00          9.00            16.00
                1.960          0.444            1.563

Males             32             7               11           50
                25.00          9.00            16.00
                1.960          0.444            1.563

Total             50            18               32          100

Chi-Sq = 7.934, DF = 2, P-Value = 0.019
```

Logistic regression

The essentials of logistic regression

Logistic regression enables us to explore the relationship between a non-metric dependent variable and a metric independent variable. We should not use simple linear or non-linear regression to do this because the dependent variable cannot respond in a continuous way to changes in the independent variable.

Suppose our dependent variable is whether or not respondents to the food quality survey I used in the previous two sections of this chapter were asked, 'Would you recommend this restaurant to a friend? Yes or No.' There are only two possible answers. There is no scaling of 'Yes-ness' or 'No-ness': it is a binary classification.

If we want to look at the relationship between responses to this question and the age of the respondents we can use logistic regression. The survey data for these two variables is in Table 3.7. To enable us to use numerical analysis I have coded the Recommend responses as '1' for Yes and '0' for No. The Age data are in years.

To analyse this data I entered the data in two columns of the Minitab worksheet and from the Regression sub-menu within the Stat menu chose the Binary Logistic Regression tool. I selected Recommend as the Response, or dependent variable and Age as the Model; the output this generated is shown in Minitab 3.5. It is wide in scope so I will concentrate on the key features, which are the ones I have highlighted in bold.

TABLE 3.7   Restaurant Recommendation and Age data

Age	Recommend	Age	Recommend
21	0	52	1
22	0	52	1
25	0	52	0
25	1	52	1
25	0	53	1
26	0	54	1
26	1	56	1
26	0	57	0
27	1	60	1
29	0	61	0
32	0	61	1
32	0	62	0
33	1	63	1
34	0	64	1
40	1	64	1
40	1	65	1
41	1	65	0
41	0	65	1
42	1	66	1
42	1	67	1
43	0	68	0
45	1	73	1
45	0	73	1
49	1	74	1
50	1	74	1

MINITAB 3.5   Binary logistic regression: Recommend versus Age

Link Function: Logit

Response Information
Variable   Value   Count
Recommend 1   31   (Event)
           0   19
           Total   50

Logistic Regression Table

| | | | | | Odds | 95% CI | |
Predictor	Coef	SE Coef	Z	P	Ratio	Lower	Upper
Constant	-2.09420	1.00996	-2.07	0.038			
Age	0.0552728	0.0211197	2.62	**0.009**	1.06	1.01	1.10

Log-Likelihood = -29.225
Test that all slopes are zero: G = 7.956, DF = 1, P-Value = 0.005

Goodness-of-Fit Tests

Method	Chi-Square	DF	P
Pearson	29.2683	30	**0.504**
Deviance	34.1770	30	**0.274**
Hosmer-Lemeshow	1.7074	7	**0.974**

Table of Observed and Expected Frequencies:
(See Hosmer-Lemeshow Test for the Pearson Chi-Square Statistic)

| | | | | | Group | | | | | |
Value	1	2	3	4	5	6	7	8	9	Total
1										
Obs	1	2	3	3	6	4	4	4	4	31
Exp	1.6	1.8	2.8	2.8	5.2	3.7	4.8	4.1	4.4	
0										
Obs	4	3	3	2	2	1	2	1	1	19
Exp	3.4	3.2	3.2	2.2	2.8	1.3	1.2	0.9	0.6	
Total	5	5	6	5	8	5	6	5	5	50

Measures of Association:
(Between the Response Variable and Predicted Probabilities)

Pairs	Number	Percent	Summary Measures	
Concordant	419	**71.1**	Somers' D	**0.44**
Discordant	158	26.8	Goodman-Kruskal Gamma	**0.45**
Ties	12	2.0	Kendall's Tau-a	**0.21**
Total	589	100.0		

The Response Information is a simple count of the values of the dependent variable, Recommend. Among the 50 responses there are 31 1s and 19 0s, which means that 31 of the respondents said they would recommend the restaurant and 19 said they would not.

The p value of 0.009 in the Age row of the Logistic Regression Table tells us that the Age variable exerts a significant influence on the Recommend variable. Being less than 0.01 or 1% we can conclude that it is significant at the 1% level; if Age has no influence on Recommend in the population from which our sample was taken we would only get this sort of effect in 1 in 100 samples.

The G statistic tests the hypothesis that all coefficients in the model are 0. The p value based on this, at 0.005, tells us that the G statistic is significant and allows us to conclude that at least one of the coefficients is not 0. This is consistent with the conclusion we reached about the influence of Age.

In the case of the two p values we have considered so far, the lower they are the more effective the regression model. This is not so for the next group of p values, those arising from the Goodness-of-Fit Tests. All three, in different ways, assess the adequacy of the model. The null hypothesis is that the model is an adequate fit for the data. Since all three p values are above 0.05 or 5% we can conclude that this null hypothesis should not be rejected. The model does seem to fit the data adequately.

Under Measures of Association we have 71.1% concordance. This is a guide to how valid the model is for prediction, and the higher this is the better. The three Summary Measures of association assess correlation based on ranking the data. The feasible values are from 0 to 1, and like the correlation coefficient we used for linear association between metric variables, the closer to 1 the better. In our example the values of 0.44, 0.45 and 0.21 imply that the model offers only modest predictive capability.

Tell me more about logistic regression

It is possible to produce a regression model for the data using simple linear regression. I used Minitab to do this and obtained the fitted line plot in Figure 3.29. The coefficient of variation for this model is low (R^2 = 15.2%). The regression equation is:

$$\text{Recommend} = 0.0475 + 0.01186 \text{ Age}$$

We can use this to make predictions, for example if Age is 60 the point estimate for Recommend is 0.7591 (= 0.0475 + 0.01186 * 60). A low R^2 such as we have here means that the model is not a good predictor, but aside from that, what does the prediction actually mean? There are only two feasible values of Recommend, 1 (= Yes) and 0 (= No). It simply cannot be any other value, so the prediction doesn't make sense.

Logistic regression takes a completely different approach. The mechanics of the process are elaborate and are based on the balance of probabilities or odds ratios of values of the independent variable for given values of the independent variable. To illustrate, in the data shown in Figure 3.29 there are 10 respondents aged between

FIGURE 3.29   Scatter diagram of the data from Table 3.7 with best linear model

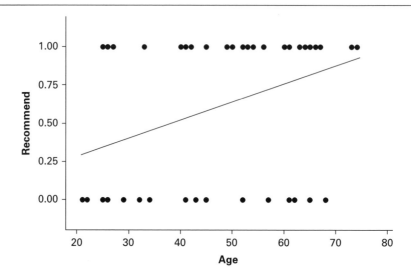

20 and 30. Of these three said 'Yes' to the recommendation question and seven said 'No'. The probability of a 'Yes' from this group is 0.3, and the probability of a 'No' is 0.7. The odds ratio is 0.43 (= 0.3/0.7) to two decimal places. Of the 10 respondents aged 50 to 60 eight said 'Yes' and two said 'No' so the odds ratio for this group is 4 (= 0.8/0.2). The odds ratios are dramatically different between the two age categories. It is the different odds ratios across the range of independent variable observations that are the focus of the regression against the binary dependent variable, in this case Recommend.

You may be wondering why the technique is called 'logistic regression'. This is because of the next stage in the analysis, which is the logistic transformation of the odds ratios to create 'logits' of the probabilities using natural logarithms. This is done to normalize the odds ratios, to create a scale of values to make it possible to produce a regression model. The problem arises because odds ratios cannot be negative because probabilities cannot be negative. Odds ratios can be less than 1, and such numbers have negative logarithms.

Unlike simple linear regression logistic regression is iterative. This means that the best model is derived through a series of steps, each one improving on the previous one. This approach is known as the 'maximum likelihood method' because it finds the values of the intercept and slope that maximize the chances of obtaining the observed values in the data set. In contrast simple linear regression is a single step process: put in your data and you get the best model straight away.

The transformation process means that the interpretation of the regression equation from logistic regression is not the same as the interpretation of the regression equation from simple linear regression. The general form of a bivariate regression equation is $Y = a + bX$, where b is the slope. The slope tells us how the independent variable, Y responds to changes in the dependent variable, X. In the regression equation for the monthly footfall and store area shown in Figure 3.12, the slope was 4.918. This told us that for an increase of 1 square foot of store area we could expect an increase of 4.918 in the monthly footfall. The equivalent equation from the Recommend and Age data shown in Figure 3.29 is Y = –2.0942 + 0.0553 Age. To get this I have taken the two figures from the 'Coef' column in the Logistic Regression Table of the Minitab output in Minitab 3.6.

MINITAB 3.6   Logistic Regression table

Predictor	Coef	SE Coef	Z	P	Odds Ratio	95% CI Lower	Upper
Constant	-2.09420	1.00996	-2.07	0.038			
Age	0.0552728	0.0211197	2.62	0.009	1.06	1.01	1.10

But what is Y? It cannot be the responses to the Recommend question because we have used logarithms of odds ratios based on these responses to generate the model, not the responses themselves. It is these 'logit' values that constitute the values of the Y variable. The slope therefore is the expected change in the logit value arising from a one year change in Age. When it comes to making predictions based on the model we need to reverse the transformations to get something usable. Thankfully Minitab does this in the Prediction facility within its Logistic Regression toolkit. I use this to generate the prediction output from the Recommend and Age analysis shown in Minitab 3.7.

MINITAB 3.7   Predicted event probabilities for New Observations

New Obs	Prob	SE Prob	95% CI
1	0.720270	0.0757462	(0.552051, 0.843254)

Values of Predictors for New Observations
New Obs	Age
1	55

I wanted a prediction of the responses to the recommendation question from 55-year-olds, which is why the number 55 appears in the last line of the output. Above that, in the third line of output under 'Prob' is the figure 0.720270. This is the probability that a 55-year-old will answer 'Yes' to the question. Another way of interpreting this is as the predicted proportion of 55-year-olds that would answer 'Yes'.

We have concentrated here on Binary Logistic Regression. Minitab also offers Ordinal and Nominal Logistic Regression facilities. These are designed for dependent variables with more than two categories. Ordinal applies when there is a logical order to the categories eg economy, business and first class air travel. Nominal applies when there is no such order.

Logistic Regression is a large subject and has important applications in a number of fields, especially medicine. If you want to find out more about it I suggest you start with Pampel (2000), which is a very good accessible guide. For a more thorough treatment I would recommend Hosmer *et al* (2013), which is in my view the most authoritative text on the subject.

Analysing multivariate data with dependency

04

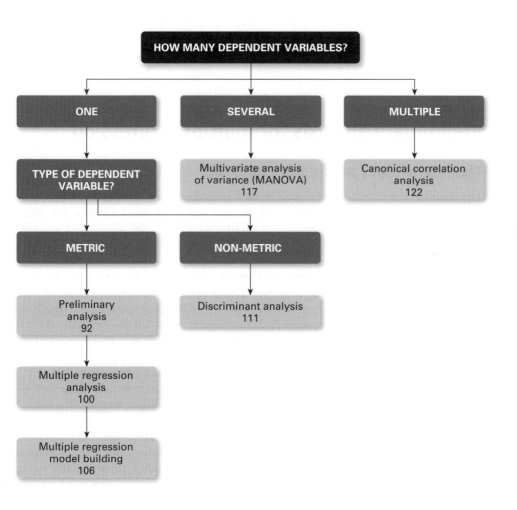

HOW MANY DEPENDENT VARIABLES?

ONE

SEVERAL

MULTIPLE

TYPE OF DEPENDENT VARIABLE?

Multivariate analysis of variance (MANOVA)
117

Canonical correlation analysis
122

METRIC

NON-METRIC

Preliminary analysis
92

Discriminant analysis
111

Multiple regression analysis
100

Multiple regression model building
106

Preliminary analysis for multiple regression

The essentials of preliminary analysis

The purpose of multiple regression analysis is to find out how one dependent variable is related to more than one independent variable – there is one Y variable but more than one X variable. Multiple regression analysis is appropriate when the Y variable is metric. The X variables can be non-metric but must be in numerical form, for example the values of a binary variable can be 0 and 1 but not Yes and No.

Before using multiple regression analysis it is important to scrutinize the data using univariate and bivariate analysis. This helps us understand the nature of the variables, especially their central tendency, spread and any skewedness, which we can assess using summary measures and diagrams. If you want to cook a good meal you would check your ingredients, and this is effectively what we are doing when we undertake preliminary analysis of this kind.

Once we have looked at each variable on its own we need to explore how each independent variable is associated by itself with the dependent variable. For this we use scatter diagrams and correlation analysis. The understanding we gain from doing this helps interpret the results of multiple regression analysis.

Next we should investigate how each independent variable might be associated with each other independent variable. Again we use scatter diagrams and correlation analysis. What we need to look for is evidence of any one independent variable being closely associated with another. If this happens the effect they will have on the dependent variable in a multiple regression model will overlap. This is the problem known as 'multicollinearity' and effectively renders one of the variables useless. By all means include both variables in your multiple regression modelling but expect one of them to have a very weak role.

Tell me more about preliminary analysis

To give you more idea about the processes you should follow before applying multiple regression analysis I'll expand the monthly footfall example I have used in previous chapters. Suppose we want to investigate what factors influence the numbers of people visiting shops. There is a major UK database company that does this for serious money so it is not a trivial issue.

What might affect how many people visit a shop? We used one factor to illustrate simple linear regression in the last chapter: the area of the shop in square feet. What else might be important? Perhaps the number of staff working in the shop as this might affect how well customers are served. Area and staff numbers are probably variables that correlate positively with footfall. Sales in shops have been hit by online shopping so we could include a variable that reflects the impact of internet trade on that market, for instance the high impact on high street travel agents and the lesser impact on clothing stores. We'll use these variables, but there are others of potential value, for instance how long the shop has been in its current premises. A long-established shop may have a greater reputation and hence attract more customers.

In our original sample there were 68 city centre shops and we had monthly footfall data for each of them. To this data set I have added figures for the area of the shops in square feet, the number of staff and a measure of internet sales growth in the goods and/or services the shop offers. This last variable has three possible values: 1 for low growth, 2 for medium growth and 3 for high growth. The complete data set is shown in Table 4.1.

For our first step in preliminary analysis I used Minitab to produce dotplots for the four variables in our data set. These are Figures 4.1, 4.2, 4.3 and 4.4. In a dotplot each observation is represented by a dot, which makes it a useful tool for showing clusters of data within distributions.

FIGURE 4.1   Dotplot of the monthly footfall of 68 city centre shops

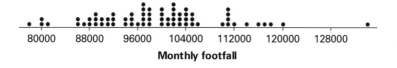

FIGURE 4.2   Dotplot of the areas of 68 city centre shops

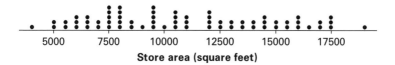

TABLE 4.1 Example data set for multiple regression analysis

Row	Footfall	Area	Staff	Internet sales growth
1	77,967	4,028	6	3
2	79,507	5,780	12	1
3	79,724	8,095	10	2
4	80,638	6,290	17	3
5	85,716	14,500	12	2
6	86,397	5,910	16	1
7	86,866	9,374	16	3
8	87,519	5,810	15	3
9	87,990	6,869	18	2
10	89,319	8,166	14	1
11	89,434	5,217	18	2
12	89,488	7,287	22	2
13	90,108	9,360	21	2
14	90,341	7,604	18	1
15	90,753	10,932	14	3
16	90,992	5,180	16	2
17	91,657	9,182	15	2
18	91,790	7,454	18	3
19	91,918	8,580	12	2
20	94,353	10,715	17	2
21	94,459	5,715	18	1
22	94,669	11,758	10	3
23	94,992	7,819	19	2

TABLE 4.1 *continued*

Row	Footfall	Area	Staff	Internet sales growth
24	95,395	8,039	14	2
25	95,773	9,297	17	3
26	96,915	5,417	23	2
27	97,123	10,545	15	2
28	97,218	17,300	20	2
29	97,230	13,019	24	1
30	97,318	7,175	17	2
31	97,607	12,194	22	1
32	97,772	9,925	17	3
33	98,021	11,110	14	2
34	98,375	10,396	18	3
35	99,847	9,499	21	1
36	100,092	7,520	17	2
37	100,260	15,882	11	2
38	100,420	10,990	15	2
39	100,663	6,716	14	1
40	101,195	12,577	18	2
41	101,570	7,581	16	2
42	102,029	12,685	15	2
43	102,201	9,710	16	2
44	102,274	13,875	14	1
45	102,319	7,964	17	2
46	102,536	12,099	22	1

TABLE 4.1 *continued*

Row	Footfall	Area	Staff	Internet sales growth
47	103,068	15,584	17	1
48	103,253	17,726	18	1
49	104,063	6,514	15	3
50	104,108	13,113	20	2
51	104,240	14,501	18	3
52	104,433	8,574	26	2
53	104,738	13,703	19	2
54	104,837	16,887	20	1
55	105,153	14,092	18	3
56	105,890	14,425	22	1
57	109,720	15,649	15	2
58	110,760	14,826	27	3
59	110,815	15,173	19	2
60	110,976	16,384	16	1
61	111,131	13,587	13	1
62	112,021	10,526	27	3
63	114,046	15,904	11	2
64	116,027	17,029	20	1
65	117,047	16,225	30	3
66	118,181	19,080	15	1
67	119,509	11,850	21	2
68	133,828	17,334	24	1

FIGURE 4.3 Dotplot of the number of staff in 68 city centre shops

Number of staff

FIGURE 4.4 Dotplot of the internet sales growth in areas of business of 68 city centre shops

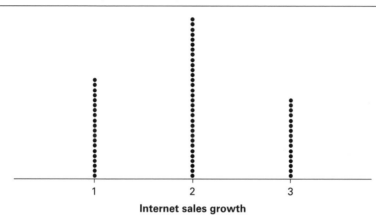

Internet sales growth

These dotplots reveal the patterns in the four distributions. The most notable features of the footfall data shown in Figure 4.1 are the probable high outlier and the small clusters at either end of the distribution. The mean of the distribution is 99,244 and the median 99,111. The closeness of these two measures of location reflects the symmetry of the distribution. The standard deviation is 10,344 and the range 55,861, demonstrating the spread of the distribution.

Figure 4.2 shows the distribution of areas. This is approximately symmetrical, with mean and median of 10,909 and 10,536 respectively, and is widely spread with a standard deviation of 3,880 and a range of 15,052. The distribution of staff numbers in Figure 4.3 is approximately symmetrical; the mean is 17.4 to one decimal place and the median is 17. The standard deviation is 4.3 to one decimal place and the range is 24.

We can use something called the coefficient of variation to compare the spread in these three distributions. The coefficient is calculated by dividing the standard deviation by the mean and multiplying by 100 so it can be expressed as a percentage:

Coefficient of variation (footfall) = (10,344/99,244) * 100 = 10.4%
Coefficient of variation (area) = (3,880/10,909) * 100 = 35.6%
Coefficient of variation (staff) = (4.3/17.4) * 100 = 24.7%

These results demonstrate the greater spread in the area data than in the other two distributions. Although Figure 4.1 has a wide scatter of points the spread in the footfall data is relatively modest. Figure 4.4 shows the preponderance of modest internet sales growth compared to the other two categories. It reinforces the fact that this variable can only have one of three values.

A key reason for producing diagrams like these is to check that we haven't made a mistake in entering our data. Suppose I typed in 13 rather than 3 in the column of internet sales growth data. Instead of the Figure 4.4 I would have got the dotplot in Figure 4.5. The error is obvious in Figure 4.5, and we can correct it. This sort of mistake is much less easy to spot in a column of figures.

FIGURE 4.5   Dotplot of the internet sales growth with data entry error

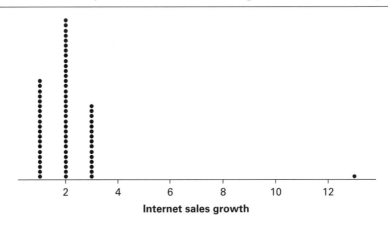

Having examined each of our variables separately the next stage of our preliminary analysis is to consider them in pairs. Let's start with correlation analysis. I produced the matrix of correlation coefficients and p values using Minitab, shown in Minitab 4.1.

MINITAB 4.1   Correlations: Footfall, Area, Staff, Internet sales growth

	Footfall	Area	Staff
Area	0.699		
	0.000		
Staff	0.451	0.214	
	0.000	0.080	
Internet sales growth	-0.188	-0.227	-0.035
	0.126	0.063	0.775

Cell Contents: Pearson correlation
                       P-Value

From this we can first assess the association between monthly footfall and each variable. The correlation coefficient between Footfall and Area is 0.699. This is positive but not too close to the maximum positive value of 1 that a correlation coefficient can have. Although the degree of positive correlation is not very strong the p value of 0.000 tells us that it is significant. We can conclude that in general higher footfalls are in shops with larger areas and vice versa.

Staff and Footfall have a more modest correlation coefficient, 0.451. Again this is positive and, with a p value of 0.000, significant. In general it appears that shops with higher footfalls have more staff and vice versa.

Internet sales growth and Footfall have a negative correlation coefficient, −0.188. This suggests that shops with higher footfalls are in markets with low internet sales growth and those with lower footfalls are in markets with high internet sales growth. Having said that, the correlation coefficient is some way short of the maximum negative value, −1, and the p value of 0.126 indicates that it is not significant.

The next step is to consider the correlation coefficients of all possible pairs of independent variables. What we hope to find here are low correlation coefficients and high p values. All three values are low: 0.214 (Staff/Area), −0.227 (Internet sales growth/Area) and −0.035 (Internet sales growth/Staff). This is good news because we don't want multicollinearity, strong connections between independent variables that mean they compete rather than complement each other in multiple regression models. A note of caution is that although the coefficients are low, in two cases (Staff/Area and Internet sales growth/Area) the p values are only a little above 0.05, the usual threshold value for significance.

Sometimes my colleagues and I ask our students to collect data about the housing market. We want them to investigate what factors influence the price of houses. Some students use the number of rooms as one independent variable and the total area of the property as another. Often there is multicollinearity between these two variables. When they combine them in their regression models they find that only one of the variables is significant, although individually each of them has a positive correlation with house price.

A scatter diagram is a key adjunct to a correlation coefficient: it tells us the pictorial story behind the coefficient. We have considered six correlation coefficients in our preliminary analysis. Rather than looking at six scatter diagrams separately I used Minitab to produce the matrix plot in Figure 4.6. This consists of 12 scatter diagrams, each of the six possible pairings of the four variables plotted both ways round. The diagram on the left of the top row has Footfall on the vertical axis and Area on the horizontal axis. The diagram on the left of the second row shows the same data with Area on the vertical axis and Footfall on the horizontal. Both diagrams have an upward sloping pattern, reflecting the correlation coefficient of 0.699 between the two variables.

The middle diagram in the second row has Area on the vertical axis and Staff on the horizontal axis. The same data is plotted the other way round, with Staff on the vertical axis and Area on the horizontal in the middle diagram of the third row. The correlation coefficient between these variables was only 0.214, hence the lack of any clear visual evidence of association in these diagrams. The diagrams down the right-hand column and those along the fourth row have columns and rows of points

FIGURE 4.6 Matrix plot of Footfall, Area, Staff and Internet sales growth

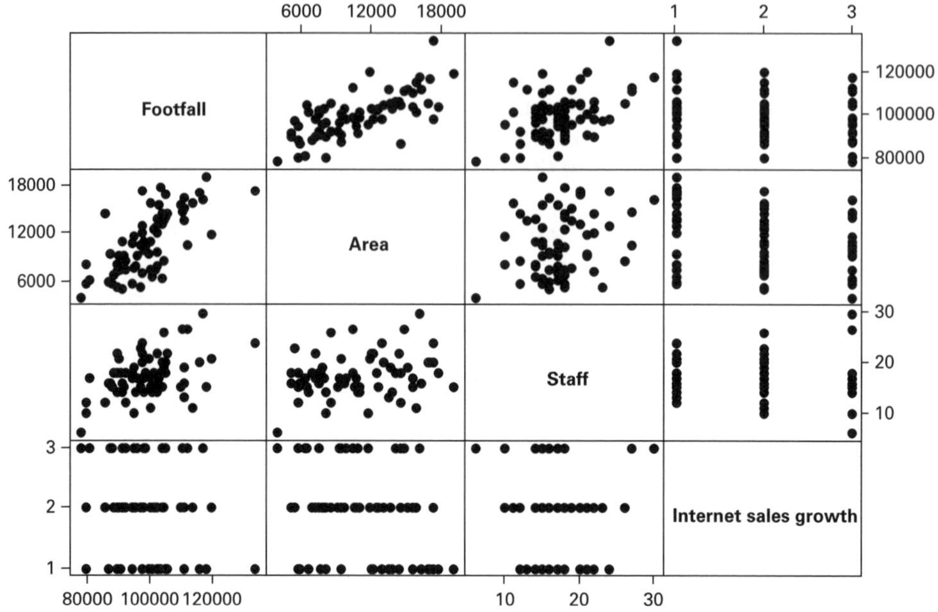

respectively. This is because they all feature the Internet sales growth variable, which has only three possible values.

The key conclusions from our preliminary analysis are that Area seems to be the most useful variable for explaining variation in Footfall, with Staff also of potential use. There is no significant multicollinearity in the data. I have called this 'preliminary analysis' because it is the preparation for building multiple regression models. We might have a clear picture from it of what variables are like but we now need to establish the best way of putting them together to explain the variation in Footfall.

Multiple regression analysis

The essentials of multiple regression analysis

The basic form of multiple regression analysis involves identifying the dependent variable and the independent variables. There is no prioritization of independent variables; at the outset they are all treated as of equal potential usefulness.

I used Minitab to produce a multiple regression analysis of the shops data with monthly footfall as the dependent variable and store area, number of staff and internet sales growth as the independent variables. I obtained the output shown in Minitab 4.2.

MINITAB 4.2   Regression analysis: Footfall versus Area, Staff, Internet
sales growth

The regression equation is
Footfall
= 68919 + 1.66 Area + 758 Staff - 499 Internet sales growth   **(1)**

Predictor	Coef	SE Coef	T	P	
Constant	68919	4730	14.57	0.000	**(3)**
Area	1.6610	0.2255	7.37	0.000	**(3)**
Staff	757.9	197.1	3.85	0.000	**(3)**
Internet sales growth	-499	1171	-0.43	0.671	**(3)**

S = 6818.16   R-Sq = 58.5%   R-Sq(adj) = 56.5%   **(4)**

Analysis of Variance

Source	DF	SS	MS	F	P	
Regression	3	4193099393	1397699798	30.07	0.000	**(2)**
Residual Error	64	2975190590	46487353			
Total	67	7168289983				

Source	DF	Seq SS
Area	1	3499202756
Staff	1	685437838
Internet sales growth	1	8458799

Unusual Observations

Obs	Area	Footfall	Fit	SE Fit	Residual	St Resid
5	14500	85716	101099	1691	-15383	-2.33R
28	17300	97218	111813	1662	-14596	-2.21R
49	6514	104063	89609	1640	14454	2.18R
65	16225	117047	117108	3027	-61	-0.01 X
67	11850	119509	103519	1088	15990	2.38R
68	17334	133828	115401	2055	18427	2.83R

R denotes an observation with a large standardized residual.
X denotes an observation whose X value gives it large leverage.

The regression equation at (1) near the top of the output is the best fit regression
model for the data. It tells us how the dependent variable is most effectively related
to the other variables. In this case we can predict that from a starting point of 68,919
the monthly footfall of a shop will be higher by 1.66 for every square foot of area,
and by 758 for every member of staff. It will decrease by 499 for every step up from
1 (low) in the three-point scale of the internet sales growth variable.

Prediction is one of the reasons for using multiple regression (explaining the
variation in the dependent variable is the other). Suppose we have a shop with an

area of 10,000, 20 staff and in a market where internet sales are medium. The monthly footfall we would expect on average, based on this regression model is:

$$\text{Footfall} = 68{,}919 + 1.66\,(10{,}000) + 758\,(20) - 499\,(2) = 99{,}681$$

The p value in the row labelled (2) allows us to test the null hypothesis that none of the independent variables are significant predictors. The fact that it is 0.000, and as such clearly less than 0.05, enables us to reject this hypothesis and incline towards the alternative hypothesis, which is that one or more of the independent variables are significant predictors.

The next question is, which of the independent variables are significant predictors? For this we need to study the figures in the p column of the rows labelled (3). There are four figures in this column, one for each of the four predictors in the model. Each one allows us to test the null hypothesis that the predictor is not significant. If the p value is less than 0.05 we should reject the null hypothesis and consider the predictor significant at the 5% level. If the p value is more than 0.05 it is not a significant predictor. In the output above, the top three figures in the p column are 0.000, indicating that the constant, which in this case is 68,919, as well as the Area and Staff variables are significant predictors of Footfall. The p value of 0.671 in the bottom row of the p column suggests that the Internet sales growth variable is not a significant predictor of Footfall.

The regression equation in the output is the best fit model, but just how good is it? We can assess this using the R-Sq(Adj) figure, 56.5% in the row labelled (4). This tells us that the regression model can explain 56.5% of the variation in monthly footfall. The implication of this is that 43.5% of the variation could be explained by factors not in the model.

The list of Unusual Observations may provide some clues to what these other factors might be. Suppose for example that the first two, observations 5 and 28, are not near car parks. This consequent need for visitors to have to walk some way to the shops might explain the negative standardized residuals, −2.33 and −2.21, and hence the relative underachievement of the two shops. They both have monthly footfalls some way short of what the model predicts they should be, for instance the Footfall for observation 5 is 85,716 whereas the model predicts 101,099, the 'Fit'. Conversely the three observations with positive standardized residuals, shops 49, 67 and 68, may be situated very near car parks.

Tell me more about multiple regression analysis

When you look at a regression equation you may be tempted to think that the larger the coefficient, the more important the variable. The figure of 1.66 next to Area is much smaller than the 758 next to Staff. Does this mean Area is less important? Definitely not: the size of the coefficient depends on the size of the units in which the variable is measured. The units of measurement for Area are small – square feet. An increase of one square foot in the area is a very small step; these shops have areas of thousands of square feet. In comparison an increase of one in the number of staff is a much bigger step; the shops have at most 30 staff.

I can demonstrate this by changing the units of measurement of the Area variable. Instead of square feet I used thousands of square feet and produced the output in Minitab 4.3.

MINITAB 4.3   Regression analysis: Footfall versus Area, Staff, Internet sales growth

```
The regression equation is
Footfall
= 68919 + 1661 Area + 758 Staff - 499 Internet sales growth

Predictor                  Coef   SE Coef       T      P
Constant                  68919      4730   14.57  0.000
Area                     1661.0     225.5    7.37  0.000
Staff                     757.9     197.1    3.85  0.000
Internet sales growth      -499      1171   -0.43  0.671

S = 6818.16   R-Sq = 58.5%    R-Sq(adj) = 56.5%

Analysis of Variance
Source             DF          SS          MS      F      P
Regression          3  4193099393  1397699798  30.07  0.000
Residual Error     64  2975190590    46487353
Total              67  7168289983

Source                 DF      Seq SS
Area                    1  3499202756
Staff                   1   685437838
Internet sales growth   1     8458799

Unusual Observations
Obs   Area  Footfall     Fit  SE Fit  Residual  St Resid
  5   14.5     85716  101099    1691    -15383     -2.33R
 28   17.3     97218  111813    1662    -14596     -2.21R
 49    6.5    104063   89609    1640     14454      2.18R
 65   16.2    117047  117108    3027       -61     -0.01 X
 67   11.9    119509  103519    1088     15990      2.38R
 68   17.3    133828  115401    2055     18427      2.83R

R denotes an observation with a large standardized residual.
X denotes an observation whose X value gives it large leverage.
```

In this output the coefficient on Area is 1661 and is now the largest coefficient in the model. If you look carefully at the rest of the output and compare it to the original you will see that nothing else has changed. The only effect of measuring Area in thousands is to increase the value of the coefficient by a factor of 1,000, from 1.66 to 1661.

Area is one of the three predictors in the model that are significant, but what exactly does this mean? A significant predictor is one that has some influence on the behaviour of the dependent variable. We use multiple regression analysis to produce models based on sample data from which we can generalize to the population. If our analysis shows that a predictor is significant it implies that if we were able to analyse the entire population the coefficient would not be 0. A 0 coefficient means the variable has no leverage: whatever the value it has no impact on the dependent variable.

In our example both Area and Staff are significant predictors and both have positive coefficients. The larger the area of a shop the greater the monthly footfall, and the more staff the greater the monthly footfall. Internet sales growth is not a significant predictor. Don't be fooled by the large coefficient, −499; the p value of 0.671 indicates that it has little if any effect on monthly footfall. This may seem odd given the prevalence of internet retailing but as with all statistical analysis look for the story behind the numbers. It could be that internet sales have different effects in different markets. In some it might increase *all* sales; customers might study the details of what they want to buy online then go out and buy it in a shop.

Unusual observations are worth some attention because they reduce the R^2, the coefficient of determination, which is a measure of the effectiveness of the model. They also raise questions about the accuracy of the data entry and how we might improve the model by bringing in more variables.

Unpacking what makes an observation unusual takes a little patience because there are several variables to consider. Let's use observation 5, the first in the list of unusual observations. We can see from the Minitab output that this is a shop with a monthly footfall of 85,716 and an area of 14,500 square feet. The 'Fit' of 101,099 is the Footfall we would expect from a shop with this area, and a staff of 12 operating in a market with medium internet sales growth, the other values of this observation, which are in Table 4.1. If we put the values 14,500, 12 and 2 for Area, Staff and Internet sales growth respectively in the regression equation the resulting Footfall prediction is 101,099. This is considerably more than the actual Footfall, 85,716, but why?

The matrix plot in Figure 4.6, specifically the diagrams in the top row, can help us address this. Look carefully at the diagram on the top right. This is a scatter diagram of Footfall against Internet sales growth. Observation 5 includes a value of 2 for Internet sales growth. This means that the shop is represented by one of the middle column of points. Based on the vertical axis labels on the right of the diagram the range of Footfall values for shops that face medium Internet sales growth, 2 on the scale we have used, stretches from about 80,000 to about 120,000. The Footfall for observation 5 at 85,716 is within this range so the observation is not unusual because its Footfall is substantially lower than the other observations that include a 2 for Internet sales growth.

The small size of the individual diagrams in Figure 4.6 makes spotting the points representing observation 5 tricky so I have included the other two scatters we need to look at as individual plots. Figure 4.7 shows the scatter of Footfall and Staff. Observation 5 included a value of 12 for the number of staff. If you look carefully

FIGURE 4.7   Scatter diagram of Monthly footfall and Number of staff

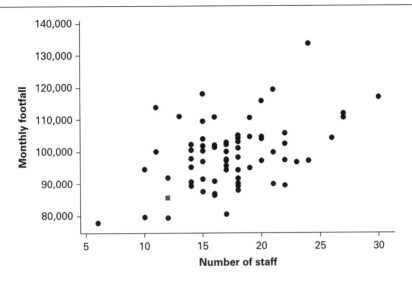

FIGURE 4.8   Scatter diagram of Monthly footfall and Store area

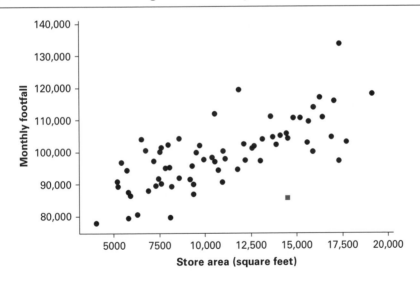

you should see that there are three shops with 12 staff, and one is represented by a small grey square. This is observation 5. One of the other shops with 12 staff has a smaller monthly footfall, at about 80,000, than observation 5. This means that observation 5 is not unusual because it has a substantially lower monthly footfall than other shops with the same number of staff.

Figure 4.8 shows the scatter of Footfall against Area. Observation 5 is represented by the grey square. It is positioned considerably lower than the other shops with a similar Area. Another way of putting this is that for its relatively large area it is achieving a much lower than expected monthly footfall. It is this that makes observation 5 unusual.

Now we have established that observation 5 is unusual we should explore why this might be. Have the values been measured, recorded and entered correctly? If so, has the definition of the measurement been applied to this shop as it has to others? Perhaps there is an anomaly; the Area figure might include a customer parking area for this shop but the Area figures for other shops with customer parking have not included it in their Area figures. Perhaps there is something specific about the shop that marks it out. It could for example be a carpet shop and therefore have a large area to display large rolls of carpet. In which case it is the size of the merchandise compared to say books and magazines that makes the Area disproportionately large.

Multiple regression analysis is a large topic area that encompasses a variety of model types. Here I have concentrated on linear models, which are usually the starting point in multiple regression analysis. If you want to find out about other model types, Gelman and Hill (2007) is a good specialist text.

Multiple regression model-building

The essentials of model-building

In the last section we considered how to produce a multiple regression model by specifying one dependent and several independent variables. Multiple regression results can demonstrate that some independent variables are more important than others.

What I call 'all-in' multiple regression is where we use every variable produces the best-fit model using all the variables including the ones that have little or no influence. But what if the most appropriate model for our data does not include every one? The real best-fit model may be one that uses just some of the independent variables, the best subset of them.

One approach to finding this is to bring independent variables into the model one at a time. I used Minitab to apply this step-by-step method, which is known as 'stepwise regression', to the data in Table 4.1 and obtained the output in Minitab 4.4.

The message 'Alpha-to-Enter' at the top of the output is what I think of as the statistical 'price of admission'. It is the maximum permissible p value for an independent variable to be allowed into the model. The p value assesses the significance of an independent variable, in other words whether it is a useful predictor of the behaviour of the dependent variable, the Response. The default threshold p value for inclusion that Minitab applies is 0.15; if an independent variable has a higher p value it is not allowed into the model.

In our example above Minitab has taken two steps in reaching the best-fit stepwise model. The first of these, represented by the left-hand column of numbers, is to bring in the independent variable that provides the best-fit bivariate model. The

MINITAB 4.4   Stepwise regression: Footfall versus Area, Staff, Internet sales growth

Alpha-to-Enter: 0.15 Alpha-to-Remove: 0.15

Response is Footfall on 3 predictors, with N = 68

```
Step              1      2
Constant      78923  67735

Area           1.86   1.68
T-Value        7.93   7.70
P-Value       0.000  0.000

Staff                  757
T-Value               3.86
P-Value              0.000

S              7456   6775
R-Sq          48.82  58.38
R-Sq(adj)     48.04  57.10
Mallows Cp     14.9    2.2
```

results show that if we could only have one independent variable to explain the variation in Footfall it should be Area. Looking carefully down the left-hand column we can find the components of the model and measures of the effectiveness of the model. The figure to the right of Constant is 78,923 and to the right of Area, 1.86. The model in its full form is:

$$\text{Footfall} = 78{,}923 + 1.86\ \text{Area}$$

The second step Minitab takes is to bring the independent variable that makes the best improvement to the model. This may or may not be the second best independent variable at the outset; it is the one that is the most effective complement to the independent variable already in the model. In our example we already have Area in the model. To supplement this Minitab brings in the Staff variable. The figures in the right-hand column tell us that the model is:

$$\text{Footfall} = 67{,}735 + 1.66\ \text{Area} + 757\ \text{Staff}$$

Note that the introduction of the Staff variable has resulted in changes to the constant and the coefficient of the Area variable. This reflects the interaction between the three model components and is effectively a rebalancing of them rather like the adjustment that the occupants of a small boat might make when another person gets into it.

The process stops with this model. The third independent that is a 'candidate', Internet sales growth, doesn't meet the p value threshold of 0.15; admission has been refused. This is not too surprising as the scatter diagram in the top right-hand corner of the matrix plot in Figure 4.6 shows no evidence of a connection between Footfall and Internet sales growth and the p value for Internet sales growth in the full regression model was 0.671.

Just how good are the two models in the stepwise analysis? For this we need to consider some of the figures in the last four rows of the output. The R-Sq is R^2, the coefficient of determination and measures the percentage of the variation in the dependent variable, or Response that can be explained by the variation in the independent variables, or Predictors. It is better to use the adjusted R^2, R-Sq (adj) as the adjustment is intended to discount for the greater possibility of random association when including more than one independent variable.

The R-Sq (adj) for the first model, with only Area as the predictor variable is 48.04%, so this variable alone can explain nearly half of the variation in Footfall. Bringing in Staff increases the R-Sq (adj) to 57.10%, an improvement of just over 9%. This still leaves nearly 43% unexplained, but our other independent variable, Internet sales growth, can't help us as it doesn't 'make it through the door'.

The S figures in the row above the R-Sq values are the standard deviation of the residuals of the models. The residuals are the regression 'leftovers', the variation in the dependent variable that the model cannot explain. The better the model the smaller the residuals will be and consequently their standard deviation will be smaller. The S value for the first model is 7,456 and for the second 6,775, so the second model is the better of the two.

The measure in the last row, Mallows Cp, is about precision and bias. If there are too many variables in the model we can lose precision; with too few variables we can get bias in estimation, both of the population parameters and predictions. The Mallows Cp should be as near as possible to p, the number of predictors in the model, ie the constant and the independent variables. In our example the Mallows Cp for the first model is 14.9, far higher than the number of predictors, 2. The figure for the second model is 2.2, fairly close to 3, the number of predictors. If the p in Mallow Cp represents the number of predictors, you may wonder what C stands for. It is Colin, the first name of Dr Mallows, the statistician who developed the measure.

Tell me more about model-building

The stepwise analysis we considered in the last section was achieved by forward selection. This entails starting with the single most effective independent variable and adding in other independent variables on the basis of the best incremental contribution to the mode. Each one must pass the entry test.

An alternative approach is backward elimination. This entails starting with the 'all-in' model, the one that includes every independent variable, and throwing out the ones that have little or no impact, starting with the one that has the least significance. Minitab 4.5 shows the backward elimination analysis of the Footfall data from Table 4.1.

MINITAB 4.5 Stepwise regression: Footfall versus Area, Staff, Internet sales growth

```
Backward elimination.  Alpha-to-Remove: 0.1

Response is Footfall on 3 predictors, with N = 68

Step                          1       2
Constant                  68919   67735

Area                       1.66    1.68
T-Value                    7.37    7.70
P-Value                   0.000   0.000

Staff                       758     757
T-Value                    3.85    3.86
P-Value                   0.000   0.000

Internet sales growth      -499
T-Value                   -0.43
P-Value                   0.671

S                          6818    6775
R-Sq                      58.50   58.38
R-Sq(adj)                 56.55   57.10
Mallows Cp                  4.0     2.2
```

In the first line below the heading the 'Alpha-to-Remove' message tells us that if a predictor has a p value of more than 0.1 it will be dismissed from the model. The left-hand column of figures includes the components of the full regression model; 68,919 the Constant, 1.66 the coefficient on Area, 758 the coefficient on Staff, and −499 the coefficient on Internet sales growth. The model, exactly the same as we obtained when we looked at multiple regression earlier in the chapter, is:

Footfall = 68,919 + 1.66 Area + 758 Staff − 499 Internet sales growth

The figures in the right-hand column include the constant and coefficients for the best-fit model Minitab has found through backward elimination. It is:

Footfall = 67,735 + 1.68 Area + 757 Staff

Internet sales growth has been eliminated as its p value of 0.671 exceeds the 'Alpha-to-Remove' of 0.1. This is exactly the same as the model Minitab reached by the forward selection approach used to produce the stepwise regression output in the last section.

In taking the step to remove Internet sales growth the R-Sq value has dropped very slightly from 58.50 to 58.38%, which suggests omitting it has reduced the effectiveness of the model. In contrast the R-Sq (adj) has increased from 56.55 to 57.10%. This is a truer reflection of the situation: any impact the Internet sales growth variable may have on Footfall is within the sort of chance association that arises because of the variation inherent in sampling. There will be samples in which two completely unrelated variables can have a small correlation with each other. It is to compensate for this type of effect that the adjustment of R^2 is made.

Minitab offers an alternative method of model building, its Best Subsets tool. This provides less detailed output for each model it considers but it does give us the best and second-best model at each stage; the best and second-best single-predictor model, the best and second-best two-predictor model, etc. The Best Subsets output for the data in Table 4.1 is shown in Minitab 4.6.

MINITAB 4.6 Best subsets regression: Footfall versus Area, Staff, Internet sales growth

```
Response is Footfall

                                           I
                                           n
                                           t
                                       S   e
                                   A   t   r
                                   r   a   n
                        Mallows        e   f   e
Vars  R-Sq  R-Sq(adj)     Cp       S   a   f   t
  1   48.8     48.0      14.9   7456.0  X
  1   20.4     19.2      58.8   9300.1      X
  2   58.4     57.1       2.2   6775.1  X   X
  2   48.9     47.3      16.8   7506.5  X       X
  3   58.5     56.5       4.0   6818.2  X   X   X
```

Best Subsets output can be tricky to interpret because the names of the predictors on the right are written vertically. To make it a little easier I have truncated the name of Internet sales growth to just 'Internet'. The column heading furthest left, 'Vars' is short for Variables and the numbers in this column are the number of predictors in the model. The top row of numbers describes the best single-predictor model. The X on the right below Area tells us that the best of the three possible single-predictor models uses only Area. It has a R^2 of 48.8% and an adjusted R^2 of 48.0% with a Mallows Cp of 14.9 and S of 7,456. Note that, unlike the Minitab stepwise output, Best Subsets does not provide the constant and coefficient. To get these we would have to use the Regression tool.

The second row of numbers tells us about the next best single-predictor model. This has Staff as the predictor. It has lower R^2 and adjusted R^2 values than the best single-predictor, 20.4% and 19.2% respectively. It also has much higher Mallows and S values, 58.8 and 9,300.1.

The third row has two predictors. The X symbols below Area and Staff tell us that this, the best two-predictor model, uses these two variables. The model has R^2 and adjusted R^2 values of 58.4% and 57.1% with Mallows and S values of 2.2 and 6,775.1. Compared to the best single-predictor model, the R^2 values are higher and the Mallows Cp and S values are lower so this is a better model than the best single-predictor model.

The X symbols in the fourth row are below Area and Internet, so these two variables are in the second-best two-predictor model. Compared to the best single-predictor model the R^2 values are lower and the Mallows and S values are higher so this is not as good as the best two-predictor model.

The final row has X symbols below all three predictors so the best, indeed for this data set the *only* possible three-predictor model includes Area, Staff and Internet sales growth. Compared to the best two-predictor model the adjusted R^2 value is lower, which indicates that it is not as good, but at 56.5% it is only 0.6% lower. The Mallows Cp at 4.0 is equal to the number of predictor variables, 3 plus the constants which suggests it is a good model in terms of precision and lack of bias. The S value of 6,818.2 is only slightly higher than the S value for the best two-predictor model, 6,775.1.

The closeness of the values of the adjusted R^2 and S values for the three-predictor and best two-predictor models, as well as the closer alignment of the Mallows Cp to the number of components in the three-predictor model make it difficult to choose between them. In such circumstances we can apply the parsimony principle, according to which, when faced with a choice between two models with similar explanatory power we should choose the one that has fewer components. In this case therefore we would opt for the best two-predictor model. This conclusion aligns with the results of the stepwise analysis.

Discriminant analysis

The essentials of discriminant analysis

Discriminant analysis does a similar job to multiple regression analysis. It relates the behaviour of a single dependent variable to more than one independent variable. The key difference is that the dependent variable is non-metric; the values it can take are categories not measurements on a scale. The independent variables are generally metric, although it is possible to use categorical ones.

To illustrate the technique I'll use the data in Table 4.2. The independent variable is the type of transactions conducted by 45 customers in a convenience store, either Card or Cash (Transaction type). The dependent variables are age in years (Age) and annual income in thousands of pounds (Income).

Discriminant analysis can help us explore the links that might exist between the types of transaction on the one hand and age and income on the other. Before applying it we can gain some insight into the connections between these variables using a scatter diagram.

TABLE 4.2 Example data set for discriminant analysis

Row	Transaction type	Age	Income
1	Cash	33	35
2	Card	18	11
3	Card	50	30
4	Card	22	28
5	Cash	55	11
6	Cash	52	41
7	Cash	49	11
8	Card	45	54
9	Card	38	47
10	Cash	40	13
11	Cash	71	19
12	Card	32	9
13	Cash	79	24
14	Card	35	39
15	Card	34	25
16	Cash	64	7
17	Card	63	17
18	Card	62	31
19	Cash	56	7
20	Cash	64	13
21	Card	28	31
22	Cash	49	64
23	Card	21	12
24	Cash	40	5

TABLE 4.2   *continued*

Row	Transaction type	Age	Income
25	Card	47	68
26	Cash	65	6
27	Card	37	16
28	Cash	60	23
29	Card	27	27
30	Cash	60	35
31	Card	32	14
32	Cash	33	21
33	Card	25	33
34	Card	61	70
35	Card	21	27
36	Card	42	51
37	Card	61	52
38	Card	25	23
39	Cash	35	4
40	Cash	66	16
41	Card	20	41
42	Cash	57	21
43	Card	35	75
44	Cash	46	6
45	Cash	60	8

FIGURE 4.9 Scatter diagram of Age, Income and Transaction type

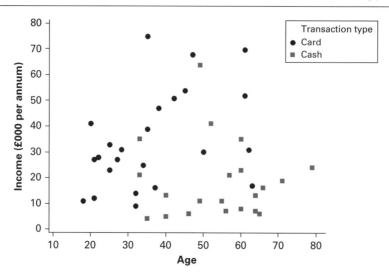

The scatter portrayed in Figure 4.9 suggests that cash transactions are more widespread among older customers and those on lower incomes. These are represented by the squares that are generally to the lower right of the scatter. Card transactions seem to be the preference of the younger customers and those on higher incomes. These are shown as the dots that are largely to the upper right of the scatter.

The contrast on the basis of age and income between those paying by cash and those paying by card is not absolute. If you look carefully at Figure 4.9 you can see that there is a 63-year-old with an income of £17,000 who pays by card (row 17 in Table 4.2) and a 33-year-old with an income of £35,000 who pays cash (row 1 in Table 4.2).

Discriminant analysis can explore the relationship between these three variables further. It produces equations with numerical weightings for the independent variables. These are called 'discriminant functions' as they are intended to discriminate between categories of the dependent variable. The weightings chosen are the ones that minimize the chances of predicting the wrong category for the observations. This is analogous to the idea of best-fit in regression analysis and the weightings are equivalent to the coefficients in a regression model. I used the discriminant analysis in Minitab on the data in Table 4.2 and obtained the results shown in Minitab 4.7.

The first section of the output, at (1) is simply the number of transactions in each category. It tells us that out of the 45 customers 24 paid by card and the other 21 by cash. The summary of classification at (2) helps us assess the usefulness of the functions in distinguishing between the transaction types. Out of the 24 card transactions, 21 or 87.5% are correctly designated. Out of the 21 cash transactions 17 or 81% are correctly designated. The card function, whose components are in the left-hand column of numbers in the Linear Discriminant Function for Groups (3) is therefore more reliable than the cash function, whose components are in the right-hand column of numbers in (3).

MINITAB 4.7   Discriminant analysis: Transaction type versus Age, Income

```
Linear Method for Response: Transaction type

Predictors: Age, Income        (1)
Group       Card        Cash
Count         24          21

Summary of classification      (2)
                  True Group
Put into Group    Card    Cash
Card                21       4
Cash                 3      17
Total N             24      21
N correct           21      17
Proportion       0.875   0.810

N = 45    N Correct = 38    Proportion Correct = 0.844

Squared Distance Between Groups
           Card      Cash
Card    0.00000   3.23516
Cash    3.23516   0.00000


Linear Discriminant Function for Groups    (3)
               Card      Cash
Constant    -4.5951   -7.8563
Age          0.1721    0.2886
Income       0.0830    0.0069
```

Tell me more about discriminant analysis

There are two functions in section (3) of Minitab 4.7, one for card transactions and the other for cash transactions. These are:

For card transactions: −4.5951 + 0.1721 Age + 0.0830 Income
For cash transactions: −7.8563 + 0.2886 Age + 0.0069 Income

These look rather like regression equations, but unlike regression equations they do not produce predicted values of the dependent variable. If we specify the age and income of a customer they produce what are called 'discriminant scores' for a card transaction and for a cash transaction. The higher the score, the more likely the transaction will be of that type. The discriminant scores for a customer aged 35 with an income of £16,000 are:

For a card transaction: −4.5951 + (0.1721 ∗ 35) + (0.0830 ∗ 16) = 2.7564
For a cash transaction: −7.8563 + (0.2886 ∗ 35) + (0.0069 ∗ 16) = 2.3351

The higher score for the card transaction tells us that such a customer is more likely to pay by card. The scores combined add up to 5.1115. The card transaction score is about 54% of this and the cash transaction 46%. The balance between these two figures anticipates the balance of probabilities for the two transaction types that I obtained and are shown in Minitab 4.8.

MINITAB 4.8   Prediction for test observations

Observation	Pred Group	From Group	Squared Distance	Probability
1	Card			
		Card	1.181	0.599
		Cash	1.982	0.401

This tells us that the probability of a 35-year-old with an income of £16,000 paying by card is 0.599 and paying by cash is 0.401. Minitab uses the discriminant functions to identify the seven cases out of the 45 that were incorrectly classified. These are listed in the output in Minitab 4.9. They are the equivalents of the unusual observations that can arise in regression analysis.

MINITAB 4.9   Summary of misclassified observations

Observation	True Group	Pred Group	Group	Squared Distance	Probability
1**	Cash	Card	Card	0.08222	0.889
			Cash	4.23844	0.111
3**	Card	Cash	Card	1.2214	0.430
			Cash	0.6563	0.570
6**	Cash	Card	Card	1.269	0.580
			Cash	1.911	0.420
17**	Card	Cash	Card	6.0743	0.058
			Cash	0.5031	0.942
18**	Card	Cash	Card	3.9069	0.167
			Cash	0.6979	0.833
22**	Cash	Card	Card	3.143	0.918
			Cash	7.982	0.082
32**	Cash	Card	Card	0.6284	0.734
			Cash	2.6555	0.266

Prediction for Test Observations

Observation	Pred Group	From Group	Squared Distance	Probability
1	Card			
		Card	1.181	0.599
		Cash	1.982	0.401

The probabilities in the right-hand column indicate the extent of the misclassifications. Observation 1, the customer represented in row 1 of Table 4.2 is a 33-year-old with an income of £35,000 who paid cash. The discriminant functions predicted a 0.889 probability that the person paid by card and only a 0.111 probability they paid cash. In contrast Observation 3 is a much closer call. The functions for this customer, a 50-year-old with an income of £30,000 who paid by card, give a 0.430 probability of them paying in this way and a 0.570 probability of paying cash.

The example I have used to give you some idea of discriminant analysis is a very simple one. The method can be applied in cases where the dependent variable can have more than two categories, as long as the categories are mutually exclusive, and there are many more independent variables.

One business application of discriminant analysis is in the prediction of bankruptcy (Altman, 1968). If you want to know more about the subject the works by Goldstein and Dillon (1978) and Huberty (1994) are useful specialist texts.

Multivariate analysis of variance

The essentials of multivariate analysis of variance

We looked at Analysis of Variance (ANOVA) in Chapter 2 as a method of testing differences between more than two population means. ANOVA is based on comparing the differences between two or more classes of observations to the differences within those classes. Essentially if the differences between outweigh the differences within then we believe the differences between are significant. The mechanics of the technique are rather elaborate, but that's what it boils down to.

We can use the same broad approach to situations where there is more than one dependent variable and we want to explore how they are related to several independent variables. This is Multiple Analysis of Variance, usually truncated to MANOVA. In this section I'll show you what I think of as the 'general purpose' version of MANOVA, the General Linear Model (GLM) often referred to as 'General MANOVA'. The advantage of this version is that the data does not have to be balanced.

Balanced data arises from structured investigations such as experiments that involve treatment groups and control groups. The investigator decides how many members there are in each group and can thus balance the data. In business projects this is not generally the case as the same degree of control is not available to the researcher. You may send a questionnaire to 50 men and 50 women but you are very unlikely to receive the same number of responses from the men as you are from the women, so your data will be unbalanced.

To illustrate MANOVA I'll use an example about health and safety employee training. There are three tests that employees have to take: fire safety, mechanical handling and workstation configuration. The test scores for each of these three are the dependent variables, although in MANOVA the term 'outcome variable' is generally preferred to 'dependent variable'. The purpose of the investigation is to ascertain whether the test scores are dependent upon three independent variables:

job grade, service, and whether or not the employee attended the preparatory health and safety training. The investigators are particularly interested in the effect of the training.

The data set consists of the three test scores, out of 100, of 35 employees and observed values for the three independent variables. We'll treat two of these, job grade and service like we treat independent variables in multiple regression, as potential predictors. In MANOVA terms they are called 'covariates'. Job grade is on a rising scale from grade 1 to 6, service is the length of service of the employee rounded up to the next whole year. Job grade and service are, for the purpose of this investigation, random variables. Training is different: it is specifically intended to influence the test scores. In MANOVA terms it is a 'factor'. The possible values of training are 0 for non-attendance and 1 for attendance. The data set is in Table 4.3.

TABLE 4.3   Data set for MANOVA example

Row	Fire	Handling	Workstation	Grade	Service	Training
1	100	90	72	6	28	1
2	98	96	93	3	1	1
3	97	74	84	1	9	1
4	97	95	83	4	10	1
5	96	95	82	5	26	1
6	92	94	82	1	6	1
7	92	93	81	4	5	1
8	90	91	80	3	5	0
9	90	91	78	5	6	1
10	89	91	77	6	16	1
11	86	90	77	2	1	1
12	86	89	77	2	1	1
13	86	89	77	4	35	1
14	86	85	76	2	3	1

TABLE 4.3 *continued*

Row	Fire	Handling	Workstation	Grade	Service	Training
15	85	84	74	1	1	1
16	84	84	70	1	1	1
17	84	84	70	4	2	1
18	84	84	68	2	9	1
19	83	83	67	5	1	1
20	83	82	67	3	1	1
21	82	81	65	4	6	0
22	82	81	64	2	9	0
23	82	80	62	5	5	0
24	82	76	61	6	3	0
25	81	75	61	6	4	0
26	81	73	59	5	1	0
27	80	72	59	2	8	0
28	80	70	58	3	1	1
29	79	68	54	1	5	1
30	78	68	54	4	1	0
31	78	66	53	5	4	0
32	78	65	49	3	24	0
33	77	64	49	4	5	0
34	77	59	46	2	5	0
35	75	57	43	2	9	0

MINITAB 4.10   General linear model: Fire, Handling, Workstation versus Training

```
MANOVA for Service
s = 1    m = 0.5    n = 13.5

                         Test                DF
Criterion           Statistic      F   Num   Denom        P
Wilks'                0.79208   2.537    3      29   0.076
Lawley-Hotelling      0.26249   2.537    3      29   0.076
Pillai's              0.20792   2.537    3      29   0.076
Roy's                 0.26249


MANOVA for Grade
s = 1    m = 0.5    n = 13.5

                         Test                DF
Criterion           Statistic      F   Num   Denom        P
Wilks'                0.75279   3.174    3      29   0.039
Lawley-Hotelling      0.32839   3.174    3      29   0.039
Pillai's              0.24721   3.174    3      29   0.039
Roy's                 0.32839


MANOVA for Training
s = 1    m = 0.5    n = 13.5

                         Test                DF
Criterion           Statistic      F   Num   Denom        P
Wilks'                0.50896   9.326    3      29   0.000
Lawley-Hotelling      0.96480   9.326    3      29   0.000
Pillai's              0.49104   9.326    3      29   0.000
Roy's                 0.96480
```

The overarching results from Minitab are shown in Minitab 4.10. The key features of this are the P values in the columns on the right. There are four tests that provide evidence of the effect of the independent variables, and Minitab provides P values for three of them. In this relatively simple example the P values for the Wilks', Lawley-Hotelling and Pillai's are the same for Service, Grade and Training. The P value of 0.000 for Training suggests that it does have a highly significant effect on the test scores. The effect of Grade is significant at the 5% level but the effect of Service is not.

Tell me more about multivariate analysis of variance

When we used ANOVA in Chapter 2 to test for differences between population means the null hypothesis was that the population means were equal, ie H_0: $\mu_1 = \mu_2 = \mu_3$, etc. In General MANOVA the null hypothesis also relates to population means, but the more complex structure of the analysis gives rise to a more complex null hypothesis. There are sets of matrices of means of subsets of values of the outcome variables by the groups within the factors and covariates. The null hypothesis is that there is no significant difference between the means of the subsets, for instance there is no significant difference between the means of the fire, materials handling and workstation scores of those who did not undertake the training and the means of the three scores of those who did.

Boxplots are particularly useful for exploring and understanding the relationships underlying the MANOVA results. Figure 4.10 shows pairs of boxplots for the three sets of test scores, one each for the employees who were untrained (Training = 0) and trained (Training = 1). The dots within each box show the position of the mean. The diagram shows higher means for the trained employees. Figure 4.11 shows the test scores distributions by job grade. Although there is evidence of differences between mean test scores for the different job grades the contrasts are not as clear as in Figure 4.10.

FIGURE 4.10   Test scores from Table 4.3 by Training

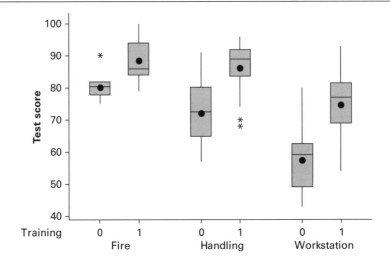

As service is a continuous variable a good visual way of exploring its connection with test scores and the impact of the training factor is the scatter diagram with groups. Figure 4.12 is the scatter plot for the fire test scores.

Diagrams such as those in Figures 4.10, 4.11 and 4.12 provide insight into the different dimensions of MANOVA results but they are not a substitute for the holistic models that MANOVA can explore. For more on MANOVA, try Huberty and Petoskey (2000), Stevens (2009) and Warner (2008).

FIGURE 4.11   Test scores from Table 4.3 by Grade

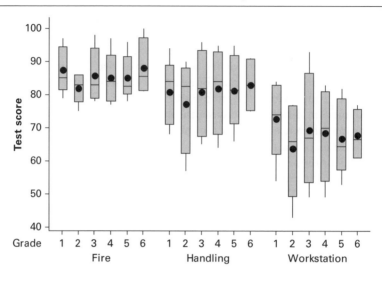

FIGURE 4.12   Fire test scores by Service and Training

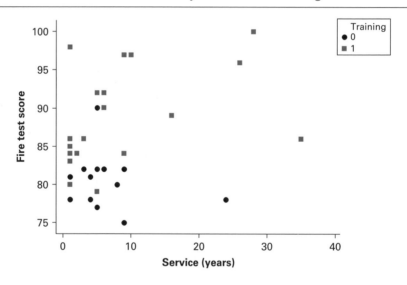

An outline of canonical correlation analysis

Canonical correlation is often bracketed together with some of the methods in the next chapter in an area of multivariate analysis called 'dimension reduction'. Dimension reduction, sometimes referred to as 'data reduction', is used to reduce the number of variables prior to analysing data using, for instance, multiple regression or MANOVA.

Why, you might ask would we want to reduce the number of variables? There are two possible reasons. The first is the existence of multicollinearity between predictors in a model. In the step-by-step model-building techniques in multiple regression analysis we considered earlier in this chapter the solution to multicollinearity is to leave out predictors that are highly correlated with other predictors. This could result in reducing the effectiveness of a model by removing predictors that may have useful, albeit possibly only marginal influences on the dependent variable. The solution that dimension reduction techniques offer to the problem of multicollinearity is to combine variables to enhance their collective impact on the dependent variable. The relationships that are then explored are between sets of uncorrelated combinations of variables.

The second reason for considering dimension reduction is if you have a large number of variables for the size of your data set. The more variables you have, the larger the sample you will need. Stevens offers advice on the desirable size of sample in relation to the number of variables for canonical correlation analysis (2009: 408). He suggests a ratio of number of observations (n) to number of variables of 20 to one or more for reliable use of the technique.

Dimension reduction can also make the scale of an investigation more manageable. A large number of variables can make exploring the data a daunting task. If you have just three variables there are three possible pairings and hence only three correlation coefficients to look at for evidence of association between variables. With six variables there would be 15 correlation coefficients, with eight, 27 and with 30 variables there would be over 400.

Canonical correlation analysis is one approach to dimension reduction. What distinguishes it from the methods we consider in the next chapter is its use with sets of variables within which there is assumed to be dependency. An example of this is customer feedback from hotel guests. Typically hotel managers are interested in the ratings guests give to the facilities and services at the hotel. There may be specific questions on the cleanliness of rooms and shared facilities, the attitudes and behaviour of hotel staff, the quality of the food, the prices charged and so on. The questionnaires used to elicit such data usually also have questions about the guests. They may ask about the gender and age of the guest, the reason for the visit, whether he or she has stayed at the hotel before, etc. The object of the exercise is generally to make connections between the rating variables and the guest profiles. To what extent, the hotel may want to know, are ratings dependent on guest characteristics? Canonical correlation analysis can help as it looks for viable combinations of dependent variables and relates them to viable combinations of predictors as well as testing the significance of associations between the dependent variables sets and the predictor sets.

Canonical correlation analysis is a complex procedure, and in my experience rarely used in business projects; the dimension reduction techniques in the next chapter are more common in such work. If you want to know more about canonical correlation analysis you may find David Garson (2012), Stevens (2009) and Thorndike (2000) useful. Chatfield and Collins (1980) offer a more technical approach. An interesting example of a business application is the work of Baloglu and Uysal (1996). They used canonical correlation analysis in their investigation of international leisure travel that involved 83 variables and 1,212 respondents.

Analysing multivariate data for interdependency

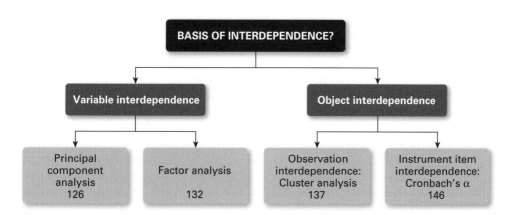

05

BASIS OF INTERDEPENDENCE?

Variable interdependence

Object interdependence

Topics in this chapter:

- Using principal components analysis to reduce the dimensionality of data sets.

- Reducing dimensionality of data sets and identifying structure within them using factor analysis.

- Analysing interdependency between observations with cluster analysis.

- Exploring the internal consistency of data collection instruments with Cronbach's α.

Principal components analysis

The essentials of principal components analysis

Principal components analysis is a technique used to explore data sets that have some structure, but not as tightly defined as we assume when we use multiple regression and other techniques that are based on the existence of dependency between variables. The starting point for principal components analysis is data with observed values for a set of variables. There is no presumption of dependency; all variables are of equal status at the outset. This might appear uncomfortably loose but in using the simple correlation analysis discussed in Chapter 3 we don't have to assume dependency either.

Principal components analysis is applied to multivariate data to repackage variables into sets of components that most effectively account for the variance in the data. The word 'principal' means main, so we can think of these components as the main features of the data. Principal components analysis is referred to as a dimension reduction technique. In the context of multivariate analysis the number of dimensions is the number of things that are actually being measured. This may or may not be the same as the number of variables. We can think of the components that result from the application of principal components analysis as the 'real' dimensions of the data. I have written 'real' in quotation marks because, like the other methods in this chapter the interpretation of the results involves exercising some degree of judgement. Since the number of components is generally less than the number of variables and cannot be more than the number of variables, principal components analysis reduces the dimensions of the data.

The terms 'variable reduction' and 'data reduction' are also used to describe principal components analysis and factor analysis, which we look at later in the chapter. Although both terms may seem less abstract than dimension reduction, in my opinion they are both potentially misleading. Principal components analysis reassembles variables into components that might involve all of the original variables. Data reduction is also problematic since the technique does not seek to remove observations or cases as they are referred to in multivariate analysis from the data set.

There are three reasons for considering the use of principal components analysis. The first is if there is multicollinearity in the data. In the previous chapter we discussed multicollinearity in the context of multiple regression analysis; it is the existence of high correlation between predictors. In applying step-by-step multiple regression model-building techniques to a situation with two multicollinear predictors, one of the two is removed. In contrast, principal components analysis takes a more creative approach by looking for ways of combining variables that are correlated with each other to form components that are not correlated with each other.

The second reason for using principal components analysis is to improve reliability. If there are many variables in relation to the number of cases the results of analysis are generally less reliable. Unfortunately there is no consensus about the minimum ratio of cases to components to achieve. Stevens (2009: 766) suggests a ratio of 10:1, ie 10 cases per component. Pallant (2010: 183) notes that a ratio of 5:1 is the threshold advised by some experts.

The third reason is to reach a better understanding of the data. By exploring the interdependency within the data and combining the variables on the basis of the relationships between them we can gain insights into the connections that underpin them. Some of these may be obvious, others less so. An example I came across was in student feedback questionnaire data. Responses to a wide number of satisfaction questions relating to their course, tutors and facilities were connected to responses to a question about the extent to which their voice was heard.

I'll use another type of feedback questionnaire to illustrate principal components analysis. Hotels seek guest feedback using forms that may include 20 or 30 questions asking for ratings of the facilities, products and services they offer. Table 5.1 is a list of ratings on a scale of 1 to 10 that were given by the first 10 of a sample of 60 guests to what in the hotel trade is usually called 'front office operations'. The higher the number, the better the rating, so 1 is very poor and 10 is very good.

A useful first step in principal components analysis is a correlation matrix. This is presented in Table 5.2. For each of the 10 possible pairing of variables there is a Pearson correlation coefficient and a P value based on that coefficient. There is

TABLE 5.1 Extract from the guest ratings of hotel front office operations

Front office staff	Front office service	Check-in	Porterage	Check-out
5	3	6	5	1
8	8	9	2	7
10	10	3	4	9
9	9	9	9	9
7	7	4	10	6
6	5	9	8	2
10	10	8	4	9
9	9	3	9	8
8	8	7	5	7
9	4	2	3	2
*	*	*	*	*
*	*	*	*	*
*	*	*	*	*

TABLE 5.2   Correlation matrix for the hotel guests' ratings data

	Front office staff	Front office service	Check-in	Porterage
Front office service	0.924 0.000			
Check-in	−0.211 0.105	−0.177 0.177		
Porterage	−0.151 0.248	−0.088 0.506	0.317 0.014	
Check-out	0.767 0.000	0.841 0.000	−0.126 0.337	0.027 0.838

Cell Contents: Pearson correlation
              P-Value

evidence of significant correlation between the Check-in and Porterage variables, and the Front Office Staff, Front Office Service and Check-out variables.

The principal components analysis of the complete set of hotel guests' ratings data set produced using Minitab is shown in Minitab 5.1.

MINITAB 5.1   Principal component analysis: Front office staff, Front office service, Check-in, Check-out, Porterage

```
Eigenanalysis of the Correlation Matrix

Eigenvalue  2.7653  1.2563  0.6784  0.2363  0.0637
Proportion   0.553   0.251   0.136   0.047   0.013
Cumulative   0.553   0.804   0.940   0.987   1.000


Variable                  PC1     PC2     PC3     PC4     PC5
Front office staff      0.570   0.057   0.060   0.552  -0.603
Front office service    0.580   0.127   0.031   0.228   0.771
Check-in               -0.186   0.658   0.729   0.036  -0.008
Check-out               0.539   0.189   0.004  -0.796  -0.201
Porterage              -0.119   0.716  -0.681   0.093  -0.028
```

In the output above the third row of Minitab 5.1, 'Cumulative' shows the percentages of the variance in the data that can be attributed to the components whose coefficients are listed in the columns of the lower table. The first figure in the

Cumulative row tells us that 0.553, or 55.3% of the variance can be accounted for by the first component, PC1. The first column of the lower table tells us that PC1 is:

0.570 Front office staff + 0.580 Front office service – 0.186 Check-in
+ 0.539 Check-out – 0.119 Porterage

The second figure from the left on the Cumulative row is 0.804. This is the proportion of the variance that can be accounted for by using both the first component, PC1 and the second component, PC2. The second component is:

0.057 Front office staff + 0.127 Front office service
+ 0.658 Check-in + 0.189 Check-out + 0.716 Porterage

Look carefully at the coefficients in these two components. We can compare them directly as the scale is the same: 1 to 10 for all five variables. In PC1 the largest components are for Front office staff, Front office service and Check-out. In contrast the largest coefficients in PC2 are for Check-in and Porterage.

The other three components, PC3 to PC5, make diminishing marginal contributions to the explanation of the variance in the data. This is demonstrated by the sequence of figures in the Cumulative row, which finishes with the 1.000 on the right. This tells us that all the variance in the data can be explained by the set of five principal components.

Having looked at the components the next step is to decide how many to use. The marginal effect of the fifth component is only 0.013 (1.000 – 0.987) or 1.3%. This is so small it is probably less than the random variability in the data, and hence not worth including, especially as the point of principal components analysis is to reduce the dimensions.

To help us decide how many components are worth using we can use either the Kaiser criterion or scree plot. Both are based on Eigenvalues. These are shown in the first row of the upper table in the Minitab output. Eigenvalues are derived from covariances, measures of variability between pairs of variables. The process, involving matrix arithmetic, is rather elaborate but the results are helpful. The sum of the Eigenvalues in the Minitab output is 5 (2.7653 + 1.2563 + 0.6784 + 0.2363 + 0.0637), the same as the number of original variables. This is no coincidence, and neither is the fact that the figures in the Proportion row of the upper table are the Eigenvalues divided by five: 2.7653/5 = 0.553 to three decimal places. These Proportion figures in turn are the ones used to determine the Cumulative figures: eg 0.804 = 0.553 + 0.251.

The Eigenvalues encapsulate the effectiveness of the components. The Kaiser criterion is to use every component that has an Eigenvalue of 1 or more. In the hotel guests' ratings example we would use only the first two components by this criterion. Figure 5.1 is a scree plot for the ratings data components. The name comes from the resemblance to the slope that scree forms down the side of a mountain. It shows the reducing Eigenvalues for the components plotted against the vertical axis. In using a scree plot to decide how many components to use we look for what is sometimes called the 'elbow' in the line. This is the point where the slope starts to flatten out.

FIGURE 5.1 Scree plot for the hotel guests' ratings data

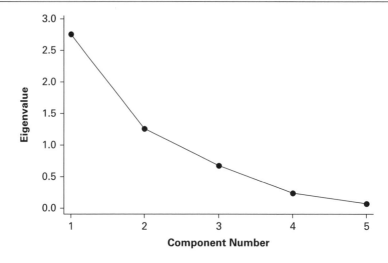

The components to the left of the elbow are the most important, those to the right the least important. In Figure 5.1 the elbow is above the position of the second component on the horizontal axis. This reinforces the conclusion from the Kaiser criterion.

The results for this ratings data are not perhaps too surprising. Guests checking in have typically travelled for some while and may arrive in groups. There is probably a queue at the desk and only a few porters to help with luggage. Guests have some degree of choice when to check out and, following a relaxing stay at the hotel, are likely to have a more benign attitude towards it.

In my example all the variables have the same scale, 1 to 10. If the variables in a data set have different scales the data needs to be standardized. To do this, find the mean and standard deviation of each variable then subtract the mean from each value and divide the result by the standard deviation. Unless this is done the differences in the scales will distort the results, and the bigger the differences the greater the distortion.

Tell me more about principal components analysis

There are two other types of graph that usefully communicate the findings from principal components analysis .The first is the loadings plot. Figure 5.2 is a loadings plot for the hotel guests' ratings variables. Each of the five variables is represented by a line that extends to a point representing the coefficients it has in the two prominent components, PC1 and PC2. The Check-in line runs from the origin (0.0) to a point plotted at 0.658 on the vertical axis, and −0.186 on the horizontal axis. These two values are respectively the coefficients, or loadings on the Check-in variable in PC2 and PC1. In a loading plot, lines for variables that have high loadings in the same component go in the same general direction at an acute angle to each other.

FIGURE 5.2 Loadings plot for the hotel guests' ratings variables

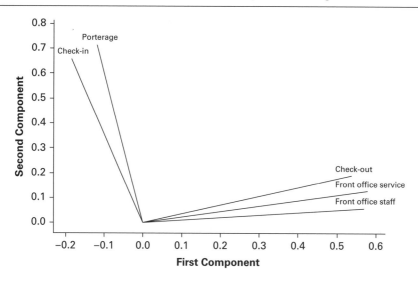

Figure 5.3 is a dendrogram of the hotel guests' ratings variables. Dendrograms, literally 'tree drawings', are part of cluster analysis, which we'll consider later in the chapter. They are useful means of conveying how a set of variables have been combined, or clustered. Starting from the horizontal axis the first clustering is between Front office staff and Front office service. This pair of variables had the strongest correlation coefficient, 0.924 in the correlation matrix in Table 5.2. They are the pair with the strongest similarity. Next is the clustering of this combination with Check-out, and finally the grouping of Check-in with Porterage, which had a relatively modest although significant correlation coefficient of 0.317 in Table 5.2.

FIGURE 5.3 Dendrogram for the hotel guests' ratings variables

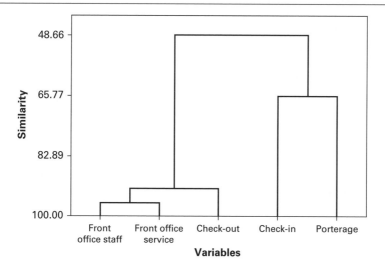

Principal components analysis is often bracketed with factor analysis, which we will discuss in the next section, and regarded by some as part of factor analysis. The two methods have essentially the same purpose, to reduce the dimensionality of data sets but achieve it through different approaches. Both look for linear combinations of an original set of variables. Principal components analysis does this by transforming the original values to increase their combined effectiveness. Factor analysis is a wider-ranging approach to identifying factors within the data.

Like factor analysis, principal components analysis is an exploratory rather than what is sometimes termed a 'confirmatory' method. Confirmatory analysis involves testing specific hypotheses about the features we expect in our data. The role of the results is to confirm or refute the hypotheses. Exploratory analysis is based essentially on general notions and broad hypotheses. The role of the results is to identify features that emerge from the data.

If you want to find out more about principal components analysis try Cooper and Weekes (1983), Tabachnick and Fidell (2012) and Warner (2008). Chatfield and Collins (1980) provide a thorough mathematical approach.

Factor analysis

The essentials of factor analysis

Factor analysis, like principal components analysis, seeks to reduce the dimensions of a data set, in other words to create from a large number of variables a smaller number of dimensions that reflect the interdependency within the data set. Principal components analysis does this by constructing linear combinations of the variables, components that account for, or 'mop up' all of the variance of the variables.

Whereas principal components analysis focuses on variance, factor analysis focuses on covariance. Covariance, an ingredient of the correlation coefficient, is a measure of the linear relationship between two variables; it is the variance that the variables share. A key assumption in factor analysis is that the total variance of a variable is part the shared, or common variance, and part the specific or unique variance, as well as a degree of error variance arising from random variation. A distinction is made between 'uniqueness', the part of the variance of a variable that is not related to the other variables, and 'communality', the part of the variance of the variables accounted for by the factors generated by factor analysis.

Like the components produced from principal components analysis, factors are linear combinations of the variables in the data set. Factors differ conceptually from components because they are grown from covariances rather than tying down total variance. It is argued that in growing them, structures within the data are revealed in the form of latent or underlying factors. These might constitute variables that are inherently unobservable. Indeed the origins of factor analysis are associated with the efforts of psychologists to measure one such variable, human intelligence.

To illustrate factor analysis I have used Minitab to apply the maximum likelihood estimation technique. This is one of two factor analysis techniques available in Minitab. The other is principal components analysis. This reflects the widely held but confusing view that principal components analysis is one approach to factor analysis. eg Pallant (2010: 181), a contention refuted by Cudeck (2000: 274). According to Cudeck, maximum likelihood has proved to be a useful approach as long as the variables are approximately symmetrically distributed (2000: 276).

The resulting factor analysis of the hotel guests' ratings data, from which the figures in Table 5.1 were extracted, is in Minitab 5.2. In producing it I had to choose the number of factors – I chose four as this was one less than the number of variables, and the point of factor analysis is after all to reduce the dimensions. This amounts to a cautious, tentative first step in the analysis.

MINITAB 5.2   Factor analysis: Front office staff, Front office service, Check-in, Porterage, Check-out

Maximum Likelihood Factor Analysis of the Correlation Matrix

Unrotated Factor Loadings and Communalities

Variable	Factor1	Factor2	Factor3	Factor4	Communality
Front office staff	0.943	0.074	0.323	-0.000	1.000
Front office service	0.995	-0.097	-0.023	-0.000	1.000
Check-in	-0.260	-0.914	0.313	0.000	1.000
Porterage	-0.121	-0.326	-0.041	0.376	0.264
Check-out	0.834	-0.111	-0.035	0.101	0.719
Variance	2.6570	0.9683	0.2060	0.1514	3.9826
% Var	0.531	0.194	0.041	0.030	0.797

This analysis profiles the four factors that have been created and how much of the data variability the factors can explain. The figure on the bottom right of the output, 0.797, tells us that nearly 80% of the variance, the '% Var' can be explained by these four factors. The first three and the fifth figures in the Communality column on the right suggest that the four factors effectively represent all the variables except Porterage.

The five figures in the Factor1 column give us the variable loadings, or contributions the variables make to Factor 1. The factor consists largely of three variables: Front office staff with a loading of 0.943, Front office service with a loading of 0.995 and Check-out with a loading of 0.834. The figure at the very bottom of the column, 0.531, tells us that this factor can explain over half of the variance. The largest loading on Factor 2 is the –0.914 on Check-in, with the next largest loading at –0.326 on Porterage. The negative loadings for these variables reflect the fact that they are rated as relatively low by guests, with median values of 5 and 6 respectively. Factor 2 accounts for 0.194 or nearly 20% of the variance while Factors 3 and 4 explain just over 4% and 3% of the variance respectively and as such do not seem to be influential.

Since we are interested in reducing dimensionality it makes sense to have the minimum number of factors that account for the majority of the explainable variance, but how do we decide the best number of factors? One approach is to set a minimum threshold for the variance, what we might call the 'cost of entry' into the model. A value that is often used is 5%. This percentage of value criterion would exclude Factors 3 and 4 in our hotel guests' ratings example and leave Factors 1 and 2. An alternative approach is based on the scree plot, which for our example is shown in Figure 5.4.

FIGURE 5.4   Scree plot of the impact of factors derived from the hotel guests' ratings data

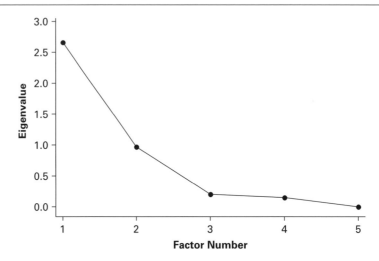

The derivation of Eigenvalues such as those plotted on the vertical axis of Figure 5.4 is rather complex but in this context they reflect the 'clout' each factor has. They enable us to apply what is known as the 'latent root' approach to selecting factors. According to this, only factors that have Eigenvalues of more than 1 should be retained. Looking at Figure 5.4, only the first two factors appear to satisfy this criterion.

The results of our factor analysis look quite abstract, so let's consider them in context. The data we have used was hotel guests' ratings of five aspects of customer service. The question we need to ask is whether the results make sense. To put it another way, what have been exposed as the latent factors lurking within the data? What's more, do these latent factors make sense? The first factor brought together the Front office staff, Front office service and Check-out variables. The first two are probably based on guests' overall impressions of the front office and the third what was probably their final experience of their hotel stay. By this time they would have most likely enjoyed their stay, but more importantly be more comfortable with the hotel; they know their way around and have probably been greeted by what have become the familiar faces of the front office staff. Factor 1 is what we might call the final guest experience of the front office. Factor 2 brought together the Check-in and Porterage variables. Since these are based on when guests arrive we might call this the arrival experience of the front office.

Reflecting on the results in this way is an important part of factor analysis. The method involves making judgements at several stages and a contextual appraisal of the results is one of these judgements. It bookends the rationale for using factor analysis, which is that meaningful factors do exist. In statistical terms there is no point in using it if the variables we have are uncorrelated.

Tell me more about factor analysis

If the factors that are derived don't make sense it is possible to derive alternative loadings by applying a technique called 'rotation'. I compare it to the operation of a kaleidoscope, a tube containing mirrors and different coloured pieces of glass. When you look into it you see reflections of the glass pieces that form patterns. Rotating the tube moves the pieces around and different patterns appear.

There are several different rotation techniques. A common one is varimax, in which the loadings are adjusted so they are as close to 0 or as far away from 0 as possible ie as near as possible to 0, −1 or +1. The object of the exercise is to produce a 'cleaner' set of loadings. In practice it would probably be a fluke to get all loadings precisely 0, −1 or +1 and stretching some loadings will affect the others so a neat, clean solution is elusive.

I used Minitab to generate the factor analysis in Minitab 5.3. I set the number of factors at two, as the conclusion from the preliminary factor analysis suggested that this was the best number to have.

The first thing to note from this output is that the share of the total variance accounted for by these two factors is about two-thirds, 0.654. This drop from the previous figure is because we have excluded two of the four factors. The two factors still have the same dominant variables; Front office staff, Front office service and Check-out for Factor 1, and Porterage and Check-in for Factor 2.

Comparing the 10 factor loadings in the unrotated results with their equivalents after rotation, six have been moved closer to the nearest 'ideal' value of 0, −1 or +1. These are the figures highlighted in bold in the rotated results. The other four have actually moved further away from the nearest ideal value.

The rotated results were derived in seven steps, or iterations. The marginal impacts of these diminish until no further improvement is available. The fact that in this case we can have seven different sets of loadings for our choice of two factors using only one factor allocation, or factor extraction approach – maximum likelihood, illustrates why I am uneasy about the usefulness of factor analysis. SPSS, which has a more extensive factor analysis menu than Minitab offers a selection of seven different factor extraction methods. For rotation Minitab offers a selection of four methods. All these alternatives not only make using factor analysis challenging but also produce the conundrum that different researchers can produce different factor analysis results from the same data. Cudeck justifiably describes factor analysis as 'a collection of methods' (2000: 265).

I have another reservation about factor analysis. It can produce apparently convincing results when there is little other evidence to justify them. To illustrate this I used Minitab to generate 60 values of five random variables each of which had whole number values in the range 1 to 10. This is exactly the same size and

MINITAB 5.3   Factor analysis: factors set at two

Maximum Likelihood Factor Analysis of the Correlation Matrix

Unrotated Factor Loadings and Communalities

Variable	Factor1	Factor2	Communality
Front office staff	0.924	-0.109	0.865
Front office service	1.000	-0.000	1.000
Check-in	-0.177	0.445	0.229
Porterage	-0.088	0.674	0.462
Check-out	0.841	0.068	0.712
Variance	2.5999	0.6689	3.2688
% Var	0.520	0.134	0.654

Rotated Factor Loadings and Communalities
Varimax Rotation

Variable	Factor1	Factor2	Communality
Front office staff	0.905	-0.217	0.865
Front office service	0.993	-0.118	1.000
Check-in	**-0.123**	**0.463**	0.229
Porterage	**-0.007**	**0.680**	0.462
Check-out	**0.843**	**-0.032**	0.712
Variance	2.5306	0.7381	3.2688
% Var	0.506	0.148	0.654

dimensionality as the hotel guests' ratings data. Given they are randomly generated variables the correlation coefficients between them are low, as Table 5.3 shows.

When I used the Minitab factor analysis facility on this data I obtained the results in Minitab 5.4.

In contrast to the correlation matrix, which suggests very little connection between the variables, factor analysis indicates that there are underlying factors that can explain 0.64 of the variance. This confounds what I would argue is the more reliable evidence of the correlation and illustrates how factor analysis can make something out of nothing. It can amount to no more than a fishing expedition in a set of data within which there is little or no interdependency, a quest for an elusive empirical pot of gold at the end of the research rainbow. It could reveal useful nuggets or simply fool's gold.

If you want to know more about factor analysis try the works of Cooper and Weekes (1983), Hair *et al* (2009), Stevens (2009), Tabachnick and Fidell (2012), Warner (2008) and Wright and Villalba (2012). Chatfield and Collins provide a useful summary of the drawbacks of factor analysis (1980: 88–9).

TABLE 5.3 Correlation matrix for five randomly generated variables

	Random 1	Random 2	Random 3	Random 4
Random 2	0.122 0.353			
Random 3	0.130 0.324	0.050 0.705		
Random 4	−0.086 0.516	0.175 0.180	0.001 0.991	
Random 5	0.046 0.726	0.121 0.358	0.144 0.273	0.066 0.614

Cell Contents: Pearson correlation
                P-Value

MINITAB 5.4   Factor analysis: Random 1 – 5

```
Maximum Likelihood Factor Analysis of the Correlation Matrix


Unrotated Factor Loadings and Communalities

Variable   Factor1   Factor2   Factor3   Factor4   Communality
Random 1    0.208    -0.181    -0.961     0.000         1.000
Random 2    0.931    -0.338     0.138    -0.000         1.000
Random 3   -0.382    -0.923    -0.044     0.000         1.000
Random 4    0.145    -0.065     0.133    -0.315         0.142
Random 5    0.064    -0.182     0.000    -0.141         0.057

Variance   1.0812    1.0362    0.9626    0.1191        3.1991
% Var       0.216     0.207     0.193     0.024         0.640
```

Cluster analysis

The essentials of cluster analysis

The key difference between cluster analysis and the techniques we have considered previously in this chapter is the starting point. Principal components analysis and factor analysis begin with the variables in the data set whereas most cluster analysis begins with the cases, or observations. It builds from the individual observations of the variables. Having said that, like factor analysis cluster analysis is a collection of methods rather than a single one, and this collection includes clustering from a base of variables as well as clustering from a base of observations.

The purpose of cluster analysis is to explore ways of subdividing data sets into clusters or groups that are similar in nature and distinct from other clusters. The approach it uses we could describe as 'freeform' or 'emergent' in that it isn't based on predefined classifications; the classifications that emerge from the data are described as 'unsupervised'.

There is considerable judgement involved in using cluster analysis, in the selection of methods and variations within methods and in deciding the appropriate number of clusters. It can provide new insights into data but it is important to consider the validity and usefulness of the results, and whether they make sense in the context.

Conceptually cluster analysis is relatively straightforward. To illustrate what it is about I'll extend the hotel guest feedback example used previously in this chapter. Suppose the hotel surveys its guests using an online questionnaire in the immediate aftermath of their visit. One issue in this type of data capture is the time it takes respondents to complete the questionnaire. Hotel management usually want to improve the response rate, the proportion of guests that do complete the questionnaire, and one way of doing this is to make it easier and quicker for respondents to complete.

The scatter plot in Figure 5.5 shows the completion times plotted against the overall rating of the hotel for 22 guests who completed the questionnaire. My purpose in plotting the data in this way is not to proceed to regression analysis, which would require some assumption of dependency, but to find any visual evidence of clusters. There are five points to the upper left of the plot that seem detached from the larger grouping to the bottom right. There is one point to the bottom left, representing a respondent who took 5 minutes to complete the questionnaire and gave an overall rating of 2. She or he could plausibly be deemed to be a member of either of the two groupings.

Figure 5.5 only shows up the apparent groupings; understanding why clusters exist rests on knowledge of the context. In this case hotel management would probably want to know what features the five respondents in the upper cluster share beyond their relatively long completion times and generally lower overall ratings. It may be that they are guests with particular issues that they expand upon in 'Any comments' sections. Perhaps they are guests who have taken more time because they are elderly or do not have English as their first language.

The example represented in Figure 5.5 is much simpler than is usually the case with cluster analysis. For one thing there are only two variables; with several variables any clusters that exist are groupings in multidimensional space, which is beyond the scope of scatter plots. Even with just two variables reliance on visual inspection is of limited use; for one thing different researchers may well see different clusters. To be more systematic cluster analysis employs methods of determining clusters based on the similarity or proximity of observations, or the distances between them.

The default approach to clustering observations in Minitab is known as 'single linkage'. This is one of the hierarchical methods, which build a hierarchy of clusters. The starting point for single linkage is to treat each observation as a cluster by itself. The first step is to connect the two closest observations together to create a cluster

FIGURE 5.5 Scatter plot of survey completion times and overall ratings by hotel guests

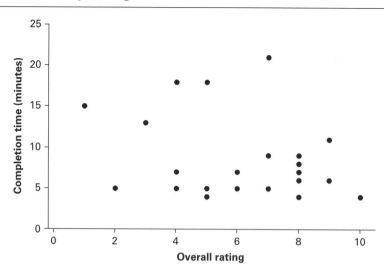

of two. The next step is to connect the next two closest observations together, although it could be to connect a third observation to the first pair if that is a closer connection than the second pairing. This process carries on until all of the observations are connected together into one cluster.

Having all the observations in a single cluster rather defeats the object of the exercise because we want cluster analysis to find clusters within the data. We have to decide what the number of clusters should be, to 'cap' the clustering at a point where it seems logical to do so. This is known as the final partition of the data.

To illustrate the single linkage of clustering observations I'll use the data in Table 5.4. For 12 respondents there are observed values of five variables: how long it took them to complete the questionnaire, the number of nights they stayed at the hotel, their age, their annual income in thousands of pounds and the overall rating they gave the hotel. Following Gore's advice (2000: 306) I standardized these variables to minimize the impact of scale differences, which is one option Minitab offers in the Cluster Observations facility I used to produce the analysis in Minitab 5.5 for the data in Table 5.4.

Each row in this output is a step in the clustering process from the first, which has 11 clusters. These are the cluster of observations 5 and 8, the 'Clusters joined' and the 10 other observations which remain at this stage clusters in their own right. Step 2 is the formation of a new cluster linking observations 10 and 4. We now have 10 clusters, of which two are pairs and the other eight are single observations. Similarly step 3 is the linking of observations 6 and 7 to form a third two-observation cluster. Step 4 is a little different in that it involves linking a third observation, observation 3 to what appears to be only observation 5, since 3 and 5 are the Clusters joined. In fact since linking observations 5 and 8 at step 1 this two-observation cluster is referred to by the lower of the two observation numbers, 5. This means that step 4 is the linking of observation 3 to the existing cluster of observations 5 and 8, which

TABLE 5.4   Results from a survey of hotel guests

Row	Completion time	Number of nights	Age	Annual income	Overall rating
1	7	5	50	34	6
2	9	1	70	22	8
3	7	4	33	56	8
4	5	4	43	36	6
5	6	3	40	52	8
6	5	6	63	34	5
7	5	6	71	26	5
8	6	2	42	50	8
9	4	2	43	32	5
10	5	3	44	28	6
11	9	5	51	26	7
12	6	1	52	50	9

MINITAB 5.5   Cluster analysis of observations: Completion time, Number of nights, Age, Annual income, Overall rating

```
Standardized Variables, Euclidean Distance, Single Linkage
Amalgamation Steps

                                                       Number
                                                       of obs.
        Number of  Similarity  Distance  Clusters       New   in new
Step    clusters     level       level   joined     cluster  cluster
  1        11       87.5041    0.60892   5     8         5       2
  2        10       81.8107    0.88636   4    10         4       2
  3         9       80.4883    0.95080   6     7         6       2
  4         8       77.8548    1.07913   3     5         3       3
  5         7       76.3403    1.15293   4     9         4       3
  6         6       74.9047    1.22289   3    12         3       4
  7         5       69.0801    1.50672   1     4         1       4
  8         4       67.1909    1.59878   1    11         1       5
  9         3       61.2821    1.88672   1     6         1       7
 10         2       55.9429    2.14689   1     3         1      11
 11         1       41.5291    2.84927   1     2         1      12
```

in keeping with the cluster numbering convention here is henceforth known as cluster 3.

By the time we get to step 11 we have all the observations in a single cluster. If this was a bus journey we have stayed on the bus too long and are now at the terminus. Where should we have got off the bus? One of the two columns I haven't mentioned so far can help us decide this. The 'Similarity level' is, as its name implies a measure of the similarity or proximity of the observations linked at that step of the analysis, although not a straightforward one. The similarity level is on a scale of 0 to 100 for no similarity and complete similarity respectively. As we take further steps the similarity level drops. Distance level between clusters is the other criteria for assessing the stage of clustering. In general the larger the distance level the less distinct the clusters and the less informative the analysis.

Deciding the final partition, in other words how many clusters to use, is a judgement of the best balance of high similarity level while avoiding so many clusters that the results are too granular. In our example I would choose four clusters because the steps after partitioning the data into four clusters are associated with a considerable decline in similarity value from 67.1909 to 41.5291.

Repeating the Minitab analysis but this time setting the number of clusters to four produces the output in Minitab 5.6, which tells us more about the clusters. The first cluster consists of five observations with a sum of squares of 10.4180. This gauges the spread in the cluster; the smaller the sum of squares, the more concentrated the cluster. Cluster 3, with a much lower sum of squares of 3.6834 is a more compact cluster albeit with one less observation. Cluster 2 has only one observation and hence no spread. Single observation clusters like this are sometimes known as 'runts' as they stand out as individual oddities.

The centroid is the middle of a cluster, worked out from the means of the observed values of each variable for the observations in the cluster. The average and maximum distances from the centroids reflect the spread within the clusters.

Figure 5.6 is a dendrogram showing the four clusters. The cluster identified as Cluster 1 in the Minitab output above comprises observations 1, 4, 10, 9 and 11 and is shown on the left. Cluster 2 is observation 2, the 'runt' on the far right. Cluster 3, to the right brings together observations 3, 5, 8, 12. Cluster 4, in the middle has observations 6 and 7.

MINITAB 5.6   Final partition

Number of clusters: 4

	Number of observations	Within cluster sum of squares	Average distance from centroid	Maximum distance from centroid
Cluster1	5	10.4180	1.32801	2.20901
Cluster2	1	0.0000	0.00000	0.00000
Cluster3	4	3.6834	0.84802	1.32690
Cluster4	2	0.4520	0.47540	0.47540

FIGURE 5.6   Dendrogram of the four clusters of the data in Table 5.4

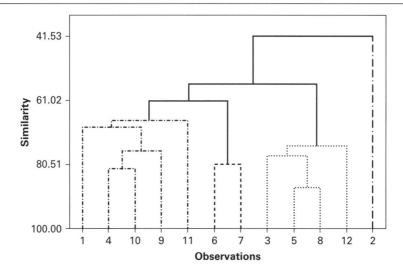

Having seen these four clusters emerge from the analysis, the next stage would be to consider the observations in their clusters. We might consider in this case what hotel management can learn from the results. Looking back at Table 5.4, Cluster 1 consists of five middle-aged respondents on modest incomes who give the hotel middling ratings. The second largest cluster, Cluster 3 consists of four guests on higher incomes who gave the hotel higher overall ratings. The contrast between these two clusters might lead the hotel management to consider for instance whether guests on lower incomes deem the hotel experience poor value for money.

Tell me more about cluster analysis

Dendrograms like Figure 5.6 are useful ways of displaying hierarchical clustering. They show the formation of the clusters from the horizontal axis, where all observations are represented separately, to the horizontal line at the very top, which marks the consolidation of all the observations into a single cluster.

The vertical scale of 'similarity' in Figure 5.6 looks a little odd because from a base of 100 the values get lower as we move up the scale. Two observations that are exactly the same will have a similarity level of 100 and will be connected by a horizontal line along the horizontal axis. The nearer a horizontal line linking observations is to the horizontal axis the greater the similarity level and the tighter or more compact the cluster they form. Conversely, the further away a line linking two observations is from the horizontal axis, the looser or more diffuse the cluster.

To illustrate how cluster compactness is reflected in the similarity scale of a dendrogram I took the data from Minitab 5.3 and modified three of the four observations that constituted Cluster 3 in the original analysis. The amended data is listed in Table 5.5 with asterisks marking the values I have changed. The ages for observations 3 and 12 are now 36 and 44, closer to the ages of the other two

TABLE 5.5 Amended results from a survey of hotel guests

Row	Completion time	Number of nights	Age	Annual income	Overall rating
1	7	5	50	34	6
2	9	1	70	22	8
3	7	4	36*	56	8
4	5	4	43	36	6
5	6	4*	40	52	8
6	5	6	63	34	5
7	5	6	71	26	5
8	6	4*	42	50	8
9	4	2	43	32	5
10	5	3	44	28	6
11	9	5	51	26	7
12	6	4*	44*	50	9

respondents in Cluster 3, which are 40 and 42. The number of nights stayed is now the same for all four observations: 4.

Figure 5.7 is the dendrogram from single linkage clustering of the observations in Table 5.5. In most respects it is the same as the dendrogram in Figure 5.6; the same observations are brought together in the same clusters. The only difference is that the lines to the right representing the clustering of observations 3, 5, 8 and 12 are closer to the horizontal axis. There is a slight difference in the vertical scale labels between Figures 5.6 and 5.7 which precludes a precise comparison of the similarity levels in the two diagrams but the earlier assembly of the cluster is evident. In Figure 5.6 the lines that bring observations 3 and 12 into the cluster are clearly above the central horizontal line linking observations 6 and 7. In Figure 5.7 the equivalent lines to the right are below this central line. This reflects the now greater similarity between the four observations in Cluster 3 since observations 6 and 7 haven't changed.

To produce the cluster analysis output above I used the default settings in the Minitab Cluster Observations facility, the single linkage method and Euclidean distances. The package has six other linkage methods and four other distance criteria. Which to choose depends on the nature of the data, for example whether there are outliers.

FIGURE 5.7   Dendrogram of the four clusters of the data in Table 5.5

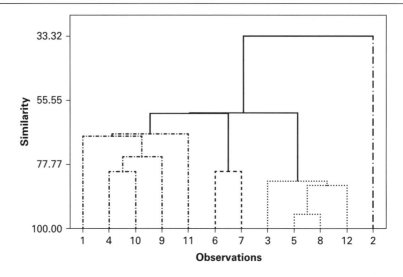

In the method of cluster analysis we have considered there is no need to specify the number of clusters, or partitions at the outset. This is particularly useful if we are starting with no preconceptions about how the data may be grouped.

If we do have some basis on which to set the number of clusters we can use another method of cluster analysis, K-means clustering. The process starts with the specification of the cluster centres, the centroids for each of the clusters required, the number of which is denoted as K. Each observation is then allocated to its nearest cluster centre. After all the observation has been allocated to a cluster the cluster centroids, which are based on the means of the observed variable values of the cluster members, are recalculated. The centroids will have changed so the allocations are re-assessed, since some observations may no longer be attached to the nearest centroid. The process continues until convergence, ie the point at which further reallocation is not worthwhile.

To illustrate K-means clustering, we'll cluster the hotel guest feedback survey data in Table 5.4 by the purpose for which the guests stayed at the hotel. This may help hotel management shape their marketing strategy. Suppose that purpose of visit was not one of the questions posed in the feedback questionnaire but we do know that observation 5 is data from a guest whose purpose of visit was business, observation 6 is from a guest staying for social reasons eg to attend a wedding, and observation 10 is from a guest staying for leisure. We can set these three observations as the initial centroids and use K-means clustering to identify groupings of guests whose profiles seem similar. I used Minitab to analyse the data from Table 5.4. The output in Minitab 5.7 is an extract of the results.

This tells us that three clusters have been identified and the number of observations in each cluster. What it doesn't tell us is which observations fall into which clusters. For this, Minitab offers an option that I used to produce Table 5.6.

MINITAB 5.7 K-means cluster analysis: Completion time, No. nights, Age, Annual income, Overall rating

```
Standardized Variables

Final Partition

Number of clusters: 3

                            Within    Average    Maximum
                           cluster   distance   distance
               Number of    sum of       from       from
              observations  squares   centroid   centroid
Cluster1               4     3.683      0.848      1.327
Cluster2               2     0.452      0.475      0.475
Cluster3               6    20.855      1.744      2.949
```

TABLE 5.6 Clusters of hotel guests by purpose of visit on the basis of K-means clustering

Row	Completion time	No of nights	Age	Annual income	Overall rating	Cluster no	Imputed purpose of visit
1	7	5	50	34	6	3	Leisure
2	9	1	70	22	8	3	Leisure
3	7	4	33	56	8	1	Business
4	5	4	43	36	6	3	Leisure
5	6	3	40	52	8	1	Business
6	5	6	63	34	5	2	Social
7	5	6	71	26	5	2	Social
8	6	2	42	50	8	1	Business
9	4	2	43	32	5	3	Leisure
10	5	3	44	28	6	3	Leisure
11	9	5	51	26	7	3	Leisure
12	6	1	52	50	9	1	Business

The results in Table 5.6 suggest that the four guests presumed to be staying for business have higher annual incomes and give the hotel relatively high overall ratings. In contrast the six presumed leisure guests have lower incomes and give the hotel lower overall ratings.

Although cluster analysis can yield interesting and useful results I share the reservations that Cooper and Weekes express about its inherent looseness. They point to the difficulty of defining exactly what constitutes a cluster, especially when the shapes that any clusters form are multidimensional. Their second issue is the uncertainty about the number of clusters that may exist, which in their view makes cluster analysis no more than a fishing expedition (1983: 315).

If you want to know more about cluster analysis, see Chatfield and Collins (1980), Cooper and Weekes (1983), Everitt *et al* (2011) and Gore (2000).

Cronbach's α

The essentials of Cronbach's α

If you use a questionnaire as an instrument to collect data you may be asked to assess its reliability. A common approach to this is to test the internal consistency of the questionnaire using something called Cronbach's α, which Cronbach himself called 'coefficient alpha' (1951). It is used very widely and in my experience often inappropriately, so I have included this section to convey what it does and its limitations.

Cronbach's α is used to address the problem that measuring attitudes and behaviours is not a precise science. In making physical measurements such as finding the dimensions of a room using a tape measure or testing the acidity of a chemical with litmus paper, the instrument itself does not change, so whoever uses it and whenever they use it, it is completely reliable. We cannot expect the same total reliability from a questionnaire. When we use it as a measurement instrument the variation in responses could reflect real differences between respondents or a degree of error. A useful way of understanding Cronbach's α is offered by DeVellis (2003: 29). He explains it as the proportion of the total variation that is the 'signal', the real difference between respondents. The error or 'noise' is $1 - \alpha$.

The calculation of Cronbach's α is complex. It involves dividing the items in an instrument, which in business projects tends to be the individual questions in a questionnaire, into two equal halves. If there are 10 questions five are taken and the responses to those questions correlated against the responses to the other five. This is repeated for every possible pair of halves eg questions 1 to 5 against questions 6 to 10, then questions 1 to 4 and 6 against questions 5 and 7 to 10 and so on. At the end of this process the average of the correlations of all possible pairs of halves is worked out. This is Cronbach's α.

The value of Cronbach's α should be somewhere between 0 and 1. Several authors identify anything above 0.7 as reasonable and 0.8 as good, and therefore indicative of internal consistency in the instrument (Foster and Parker, 1995: 90; Pallant, 2010: 100; Rust, 2012: 149–50). This tends to be the consensus, but as Rust points out, the threshold of acceptability depends on what is being measured and how (2012: 150).

The authors of many projects that I have seen use Cronbach's α as a 'magic bullet' to demonstrate the reliability of their instrument. Often they use it indiscriminately on the entire instrument. It is important to remember that it is a way of gauging consistency. If there is no reason for consistency then don't use it. It can only be of use if there is a set of items between which consistency can be expected.

Suppose we have a questionnaire that has several rating scale questions based on statements intended to measure employees' perspective of management effectiveness. It is reasonable to expect internal consistency between the responses to these questions. We would expect high scores for, 'My manager is helpful' to occur alongside high scores for, 'My manager is good at managing people'. We would not expect high scores for these statements to necessarily occur with high scores for, 'My career prospects at this company are good'.

It is possible to get a negative value for Cronbach's α. This may arise if the items cannot logically be expected to be consistent but sometimes arise with items that should be. This is when we use what I'll call 'negative questions'. In a list of statements about management effectiveness we could have the statement, 'My manager doesn't look after my interests'. Employees who are generally positive about management effectiveness would give this a low score, which would be inconsistent with the high scores for the other management effectiveness statements. To get around the difficulty we would have to reverse them, eg on a scale of 1 to 5 a 5 becomes a 1, a 4 becomes a 2 and so on. Given this difficulty, why do people use negatively worded questions? The answer is often simply to keep the respondent alert; if there is a long list of similar statements it is tempting to keep ticking down the same column.

Tell me more about Cronbach's α

I created some simple data sets to demonstrate the 'stories' behind different values of Cronbach's α. Table 5.7 lists the first of these. Assume that 25 respondents were asked to rate four aspects of customer service on a scale of 1 to 10 where 1 is very poor and 10 is excellent.

The figures in Table 5.7 are ranked to obtain a general consistency of response across the four items A1 – A4. The correlation matrix in Table 5.8 and the matrix plot in Figure 5.8 show the high levels of association between the scores on the four aspects.

Both Table 5.8 and Figure 5.8 suggest that the scores on the four aspects are closely correlated so we have evidence that the four items are consistent in measuring customer service. I used SPSS to find Cronbach's α for these items, which was 0.989. This is above the threshold of 0.7 suggested by Pallant (2010) and we can conclude that there is internal consistency between items A1 to A4. Collectively they appear to be a reliable way of measuring customer service.

What does a lower value of Cronbach's α represent? Suppose there are four other items, A5 to A8 in our instrument. The 25 scores for each of these items are listed in Table 5.9.

TABLE 5.7   Customer ratings of four aspects of customer service (A1 to A4)

A1	A2	A3	A4
1	1	1	2
1	2	1	2
1	2	2	2
2	2	2	2
2	2	2	2
2	3	2	2
3	4	3	3
4	4	3	3
5	4	3	3
5	4	3	3
5	4	4	3
5	5	4	4
6	5	5	4
6	5	5	4
6	5	6	5
6	6	6	5
7	6	6	5
7	7	7	5
7	7	7	6
8	8	7	7
8	8	7	8
8	9	8	8
8	9	9	9
9	9	9	9
10	10	10	9

TABLE 5.8 Correlation matrix for the customer service aspects A1 to A4

	A1	A2	A3
A2	0.961		
	0.000		
A3	0.959	0.977	
	0.000	0.000	
A4	0.916	0.969	0.962
	0.000	0.000	0.000

Cell Contents: Pearson correlation
              P-Value

FIGURE 5.8 Matrix plot of the customer service aspects A1 to A4

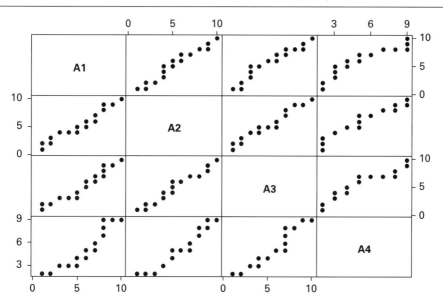

The correlation coefficients for the scores on these four aspects are in Table 5.10.
Figure 5.9 is a matrix plot of them.

Both Table 5.10 and Figure 5.9 suggest that there is little association between the
four aspects and they appear to be inconsistent. Cronbach's α for items A5 to A8 is
0.144, a value much lower than for aspects A1 to A4 and below Pallant's threshold
of 0.7. This suggests that items A5 to A8 do not constitute a collectively reliable way
to measure customer service.

TABLE 5.9 Customer ratings of four aspects of customer service (A5 to A8)

A5	A6	A7	A8
1	4	4	10
2	2	1	6
2	6	10	6
2	5	4	7
2	7	2	6
2	7	1	10
2	5	4	4
3	6	1	4
3	4	1	3
3	5	3	6
4	8	6	2
4	7	1	3
5	5	4	2
6	6	2	1
6	7	6	9
6	4	4	6
6	3	2	2
7	4	3	5
7	3	1	9
8	5	3	2
8	3	4	6
8	2	9	8
9	8	6	8
9	3	6	8
10	5	1	9

TABLE 5.10   Correlation matrix for the customer service aspects A5 to A8

	A5	A6	A7
A6	−0.207 0.322		
A7	0.146 0.486	0.043 0.838	
A8	0.082 0.696	−0.113 0.591	0.177 0.398

Cell Contents: Pearson correlation
                P-Value

FIGURE 5.9   Matrix plot of the customer service aspects A5 to A8

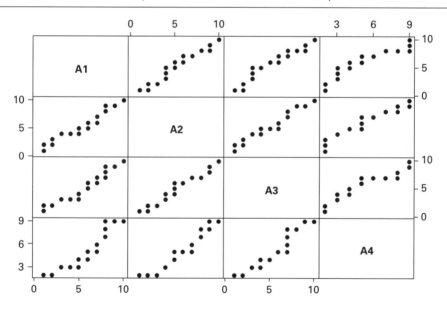

A low value of Cronbach's α will occur for a set of consistent items if one or more are negatively worded. To illustrate this I have reversed the order of the scores for A4 in Table 5.8. The amended list of scores is in Table 5.11. I have not changed the scores for A1, A2 and A3.

TABLE 5.11 Customer ratings for A1 to A4 with reversed sequence of A4 scores

A1	A2	A3	A4 Reversed sequence
1	1	1	9
1	2	1	9
1	2	2	9
2	2	2	8
2	2	2	8
2	3	2	7
3	4	3	6
4	4	3	5
5	4	3	5
5	4	3	5
5	4	4	5
5	5	4	4
6	5	5	4
6	5	5	4
6	5	6	3
6	6	6	3
7	6	6	3
7	7	7	3
7	7	7	3
8	8	7	2
8	8	7	2
8	9	8	2
8	9	9	2
9	9	9	2
10	10	10	2

The correlation matrix for the data in Table 5.11 is in Table 5.12. Figure 5.10 shows a matrix plot of the data. Table 5.12 and Figure 5.10 demonstrate a high degree of association between these four items even though I reversed the sequence of the A4 scores. Despite this Cronbach's α for the data in Table 5.12 is 0.169. This is much lower than the sort of value, 0.7 or so which, according to Pallant (2010) would suggest internal consistency between the four items. If I changed the sequence of the A4 scores back to their original sequence the value of Cronbach's α would once again be close to 1.0.

TABLE 5.12   Correlation matrix for the data in Table 5.11

	A1	A2	A3
A2	0.961		
	0.000		
A3	0.959	0.977	
	0.000	0.000	
A4	−0.970	−0.931	−0.920
	0.000	0.000	0.000

Cell Contents: Pearson correlation
              P-Value

The inconvenience of adjusting the scores of negative values aside, I have reservations about the use of Cronbach's α as a general purpose touchstone of internal consistency. I find correlation coefficients and matrix plots more useful guides to consistency of measurement between items. Having said that, I accept that for large numbers of items the consequential large correlation matrices and potentially microscopic matrix plots may be difficult to interpret and communicate. My advice is that if you do want to use Cronbach's α do so on the basis of a tenable reason for assuming consistency between the items. It is a widely used measure and as Warner (2008: 855) points out, it can be of use in refining a research instrument.

For more on Cronbach's α you may find DeVellis (2003) and Warner (2008) helpful. Interestingly, in an article published posthumously Cronbach reflects on the often casual use of coefficient α in student projects (2004: 2–3), referring to it rather dismissively as 'a crude device that does not bring to the surface many subtleties implied by variance components' (2004: 8). He goes on to state that 'I no longer regard the alpha formula as the most appropriate way to examine most data' (2004: 14) and proceeds to advocate alternative approaches.

FIGURE 5.10   Matrix plot of the data in Table 5.12

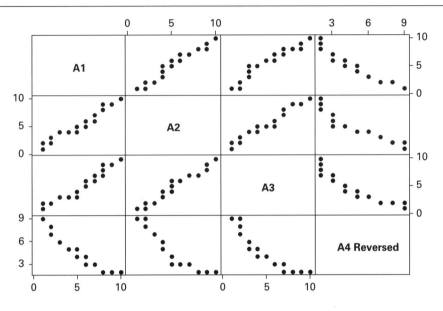

Coda
Some tips on writing up projects involving data analysis

Gathering and analysing data usually takes a good deal of time and effort. It may have been a real challenge and you simply can't wait to wrap it all up. I have read many projects where the authors seem to have gathered up all the tables, charts and diagrams and done little more than dump them in the document. This is always a pity because it makes it so difficult to reward what is often potentially valuable analysis.

Whether your project is intended to satisfy academic or commercial requirements there are several things that you can do to maximize the impact of your analysis on your audience. Drawing on the experience of supervising and marking hundreds of projects, I can offer you advice on how to do this. I should add that the advice in this section may not be appropriate for all projects, and is certainly not intended to override what your supervisor(s) tell you to do. Their advice will be based on the assessment criteria and guidelines that will apply to your work so you should adhere strictly to their advice, which may differ from what you will read below.

Writing up is probably the final stage of your project. This is months, maybe even years after you started it. The further away in time the beginning was, the more difficult it generally is to revisit the early stages, yet it is very important that you do so. You will probably have been asked to draw up research questions that your research is intended to answer. You may also have specified hypotheses that the analysis of your data is intended to address. The data analysis aspect of your work, from how you collected your data to how you present your findings should dovetail with your research questions. This is a key aspect of the quality of the argument, or flow of logic in your project. At every stage you should ensure your reader can understand why you did what you did. The quality of argument is often one of the key assessment criteria for academic projects, yet one that even my doctoral students struggle to achieve. I have no doubt that they can do it; the difficulty is that they are so close to their work it is all absolutely clear to them how it all fits together. Unfortunately they will not be marking it. They need to empathize with a reader coming to their work without the deep knowledge they have of it, like those who will be marking it.

Explain clearly where the data you have analysed came from. Is it primary data, in other words you collected it yourself, or secondary data, data collected by someone else? If it is secondary data where did it come from, how was it collected and why? Be open about any reservations you may have about the robustness of the data, for instance any weaknesses in the way it was collected or the measurement scales used.

If your data is primary data you will need to explain how you collected it. Was it, for instance, collected by observation, direct measurement or using a questionnaire? If it was by means of a questionnaire, did you test it? If so, specify any modifications you made following the test. When did you collect your data? Seasons, days and even the time of day can a make a difference. Demographically the morning customers of a convenience store are likely to be very different to the evening users of the same store. Elicitation, literally 'drawing forth' is the term used for the harvesting of data from respondents. It is one aspect of your work that your readers will probably be very keen to know.

Was the data you used from a sample or the entire population? If, as is generally the case it is from a sample, how was that sample selected? Don't be tempted to pass off a convenience sample as a random sample. Random sampling is based on every element in the population having the same chance of selection. Elicitation of data from friends and acquaintances cannot be random sampling; you don't know everyone. Be honest about your sampling. In many academic and for that matter commercial projects the samples used are not random.

At this point you may be concerned because earlier in this book I have emphasized the importance of the assumption of randomness for the legitimate application of techniques such as interval estimation. If you have sample data but the sample is not random you can use statistical inference techniques *but* it is important to recognize the limitations of doing so. Although you can't draw conclusions to the degree of confidence and significance that you could if your sample were random it is quite acceptable to apply inference to indicate the strength of findings, pointing out that the results are only indicative, or to precede the discussion of your findings with a statement to the effect that the results are not from a random sample but if the sample were random it would be possible to conclude ... etc.

In the course of undertaking your data analysis you will probably have generated far more tables and diagrams than you can conceivably include in your document. You need to decide what to include and how to include it, categorizing items as follows:

1 Is it something your readers must see in order to follow your argument? If so, include it within the text. Label it as Figure 1, for example, with an appropriate title and refer to it as Figure 1.

2 Is it something your readers would find useful to see but is not essential for following your argument? If so, put it in an appendix. Label the appendix as, for example, Appendix A and refer to it as Appendix A. An appendix is not a dustbin in which you can put an assortment of results. Make sure the material in your appendices is organized, labelled and referred to. There is nothing quite like a ragbag of oddments in a single large appendix to give the impression that the writer really doesn't know what he or she is doing.

3 Is it something that, however pleasing it is to you, you don't need to show or refer it to your readers? If so, leave it out. What will impress your readers is the cogency of your discussion and how well it is supported by your evidence, not your ability to generate large amounts of output from statistical software.

If you have used a questionnaire you should treat it as a Category 2 insertion and put a blank copy in an appendix. Having said that, practice does vary and I have observed heated arguments between colleagues about whether just a blank, a blank plus one completed questionnaire, or even the entire set of completed questionnaires should be included in an appendix. Follow the golden rule: take your supervisor's advice.

Lead your readers through your analysis in a logical way. Before you report the results, discuss the elicitation. Before you report the findings from questionnaire research, profile the respondents. Crucially, report your analysis in increasing order of complexity. For example, if you have used contingency analysis to investigate the association between non-metric variables don't start with the chi-square result; start with something simple like a bar chart. Avoid using techniques that you really don't understand; generally a well-crafted project based on relatively simple techniques is better than one where the author has presented a tangled project based on the use of much more sophisticated techniques. If you really can't avoid using a technique about which you are not confident, refer your readers to an authoritative source so at least they know you have sought to understand it.

Some of your results may be disappointing to you – perhaps the response rate you achieved with a questionnaire or results that confound your expectations. Don't be tempted to avoid the issue or leave it out; findings are findings even if they are not what you expected or hoped for. They constitute your contribution to knowledge in your field of research.

The question of ethics is an important one and you must ensure that you fulfil the ethical requirements for your project. This applies to data collection. If you use a questionnaire you should include in it a statement about confidentiality, anonymity and the limits of your use of what your respondents tell you. Practice does vary, so take the advice of your supervisor(s) on the ethical aspects of your work.

Finally, leave sufficient time for proofreading your work. This should reduce the errors in it. Ask someone you know well to read through the entire work. This is a good way of checking the logical flow and the effectiveness of the connections you make between your narrative and your results. It doesn't have to be someone who is an expert on your topic, indeed it is probably better that he or she is not since the people who assess your work, particularly second markers and external examiners, are unlikely to have much knowledge of the field either.

Appendix
Flowcharts

Chapter 1

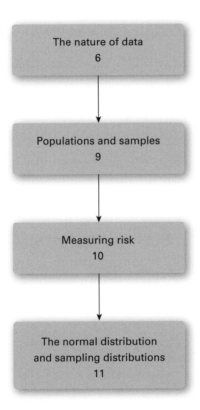

Chapter 2

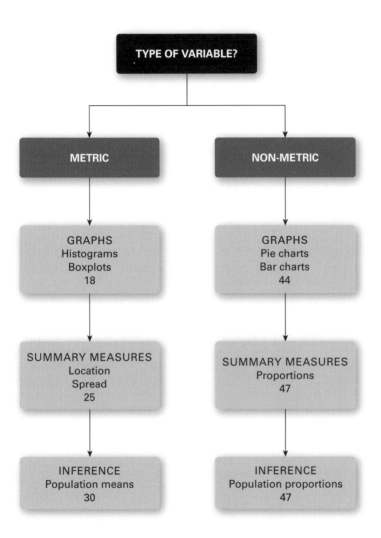

Chapter 3

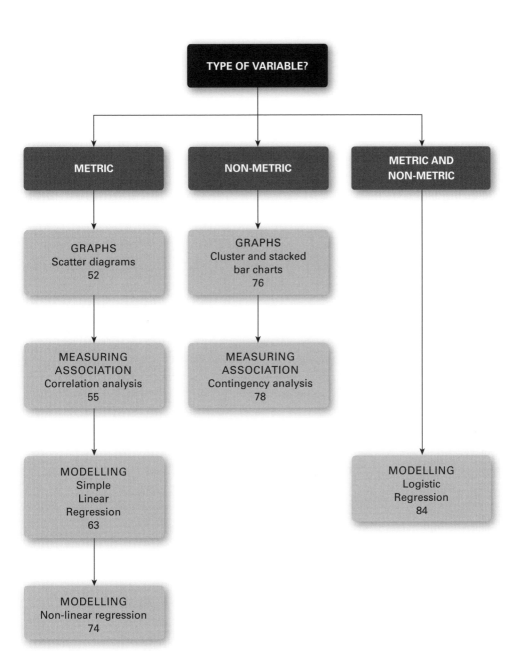

Chapter 4

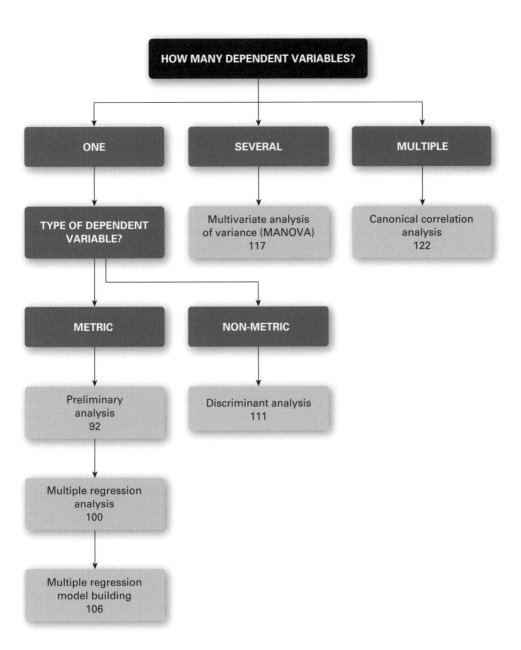

Chapter 5

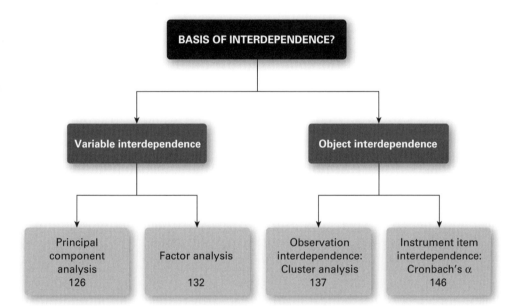

REFERENCES

Altman, E I (1968) Financial ratios, discriminant analysis and the prediction of corporate bankruptcy, *The Journal of Finance*, **23** (4), pp 589–609

Baloglu, S and Uysal, M (1996) Market segments of push and pull motivations: a canonical correlation approach, *International Journal of Contemporary Hospitality Management*, **8** (3), pp 32–8

Bates, D M and Watts, D G (2007) *Nonlinear Regression Analysis and its Applications*, Wiley-Blackwell, New York

Chatfield, C and Collins, A J (1980) *Introduction to Multivariate Analysis*, Chapman and Hall, London

Cooper, R and Weekes, A J (1983) *Data, Models and Statistical Analysis*, Philip Alan, Oxford

Cronbach, L J (1951) Coefficient alpha and the internal structure of tests, *Psychometrika*, **16** (3), pp 297–334

Cronbach, L J (2004) *My Current Thoughts on Coefficient Alpha and Successor Procedures*, University of California, Los Angeles, CA

Cudeck, R (2000) Exploratory factor analysis, in (eds) H E A Tinsley and S D Brown, *Handbook of Applied Multivariate Statistics and Mathematical Modelling*, pp 265–96, Academic Press, San Diego, CA

David Garson, G (2012) *Canonical Correlation: Linear and nonlinear*, Statistical Associates Publishers

DeVellis, R F (2003) *Scale Development Theory and Applications*, Sage, Thousand Oaks, CA

Everitt, B S, Landau, S, Leese, M and Stahl, D (2011) *Cluster Analysis*, 5th edn, Wiley, Chichester

Foster, J J and Parker, I (1995) *Carrying Out Investigations in Psychology*, BPS Books, Leicester

Gelman, A and Hill, J (2007) *Data Analysis Using Regression and Multilevel/Hierarchical Models*, Cambridge University Press, New York

Goldstein, M and Dillon, W R (1978) *Discrete Discriminant Analysis*, Wiley, New York

Gore, P A (2000) *Cluster Analysis* in (eds) H E A Tinsley and S D Brown, *Handbook of Applied Multivariate Statistics and Mathematical Modelling*, pp 297–321, Academic Press, San Diego, CA

Hair, J F, Black, W, Babin, B and Anderson, R (2009) *Multivariate Data Analysis*, 7th edn, Prentice Hall, Englewood Cliffs, NJ

Hosmer, D W, Lemeshow, S and Sturdivant, R X (2013) *Applied Logistic Regression*, 3rd edn, Wiley, Hoboken, NJ

Huberty, C J (1994) *Applied Discriminant Analysis*, Wiley, New York

Huberty, C J and Petoskey, M D (2000) Multivariate analysis of variance and covariance, in (eds) H E A Tinsley and S D Brown, *Handbook of Applied Multivariate Statistics and Mathematical Modelling*, pp 183–208, Academic Press, San Diego, CA

Pallant, J (2010) *The SPSS Survival Manual*, 4th edn, Open University Press, Maidenhead

Pampel, F C (2000) *Logistic Regression: A primer*, Sage, Thousand Oaks, CA

Rust, J (2012) Psychometrics, in (eds) G M Breakwell, J A Smith, and D B Wright, *Research Methods in Psychology*, 4th edn, pp 141–61, Sage, London

Schagen, I (2007) Why 'data' is singular, *RSS NEWS*, November, pp 1–2

Seber, G A F and Wild, C J (2003) *Nonlinear Regression*, Wiley-Blackwell, New York

Stevens, J P (2009) *Applied Multivariate Statistics for the Social Sciences*, Routledge, New York

Tabachnick, B G and Fidell, L S (2012) *Using Multivariate Statistics*, 6th edn, Pearson, Harlow

Thorndike, R M (2000) Canonical correlation analysis, in (eds) H E A Tinsley and S D Brown, *Handbook of Applied Multivariate Statistics and Mathematical Modelling*, pp 237–63, Academic Press, San Diego, CA

Warner, R M (2008) *Applied Statistics*, Sage, Los Angeles, CA

Wright, D B and Villalba (2012) Exploratory factor analysis, (eds) G M Breakwell, J A Smith, and D B Wright, *Research Methods in Psychology*, 4th edn, pp 279–318, Sage, London

INDEX